KLONDIKE '98

E. A. Hegg's Gold Rush Album

KLONDIKE '98

E. A. Hegg's Gold Rush Album

by Ethel Anderson Becker

BINFORDS & MORT, *Publishers*

Portland, Oregon

1972

Klondike '98

Revised Edition

Printed in the United States of America
Second Printing 1972

#150 02-09-2010 2:41PM
Item(s) checked out to MCCaRT, MICHAEL D

TITLE: ILL-KLONDIKE '98
BARCODE: 35394009763521
DUE DATE: 03-01-10

Deschutes Public Library
Renew at WWW.DPLS.US or phone 312-5208

Contents

Dedication

ERIC A. HEGG

1867-1948

When Ethel Anderson Becker was preparing the first edition of *Klondike '98*, she had Eric A. Hegg read the book in manuscript form. In April, 1941, he wrote:

"Dear Ethel:

"I have just finished reading your manuscript . . . . I could ask for no better supplement to those pictures which I had such fun taking some forty-five years ago. Together they will form an authentic sketch which should live for all time, gaining each year in historical value and interest. I know of nothing on our bookshelves so absolutely authentic.

"Little did I dream when your father and I were floating down the Yukon that you would some day be the means of collecting and perpetuating my photographs. Reading your story is like reliving those days when I climbed over snowbanks and cliffs, fighting for some advantageous position for an unusual picture.

(signed) E. A. HEGG"

Author's Preface

ONE DAY IN the year 1921, I stopped in to see Mr. Hegg in his studio in New Whatcom (Bellingham), Washington. The walls of his studio were covered with his choice pictures and paintings, mostly of trees and nature. Before I left I made a wager with him that I could gather together all his negatives and pictures dealing with Alaska and the Klondike. His reply was:

"It can't be done, Ethel. They are scattered far and wide."

During the years I was raising my family I always kept that wager tucked away in a secret corner of my mind. Nearly a quarter of a century had passed when I discovered about two thousand negatives of Mr. Hegg's at Webster and Stevens, photographers in Seattle. Through Mr. J. W. Todd of Shorey's Book Store, I got them. Mr. Hegg was delighted with some of the pictures he had not seen since the gold rush to Nome. It was in Nome that he and Mrs. Hegg had separated; she did not wish the wild life Nome offered. In the settlement she sold the negatives to Webster and Stevens for $250. They had calls for a few of them through the years.

Time passed. My library of negatives, pictures, books, diaries, and odds and ends of Alaska and the Klondike had grown through the years. My husband passed away in 1951 and I went to Vancouver, British Columbia, to take care of my mother. Ten years later, she passed away at the age of eighty-five.

Following her death, I went to Dawson, Yukon Territory, to review the background for a novel on which I was working. While there, I came across approximately two thousand more negatives of Mr. Hegg — left, I think, by Mr. Larss. When Mr. Hegg departed Dawson for Nome, in 1900, he had sold out to Mr. Larss, and the firm became Duclos & Larss. So the negatives bear the names of E. A. Hegg, Duclos & Larss, and W & S, Webster and Stevens. Mr. Larss carried on for a time, but when he left he decided to hide his negatives behind veneer sheets covering the inside logs of a cabin. He never returned and there they lay, safely hidden from curious eyes.

One day, many, many years later, a girl clerking in a store in Dawson bought the cabin. On one occasion she reached up to see what made the sawdust drip out of the top over the veneer. Cutting her fingers, she pulled out a glass negative showing boats going down Lake Bennett; it bore the name Duclos & Larss. Now, she decided, she could have a greenhouse—if she could get the "stuff" off the glass. When she approached her employer about it, he offered to give her the glass for a greenhouse in exchange for the negatives. She agreed.

Some of these negatives had been marked around the edges by water from the Yukon River when that stream had flooded the country. But to me the markings do not harm the pictures; they just make them more valuable.

One evening, a young couple came to the door of my home in Vancouver, British Columbia— where I was again living—and asked me what they should charge for old negatives; they were from that store in Dawson. I had to place a figure on something I wanted very badly, but also bear in mind a proper price for them to ask. Two years later I finally bought them and now had about four thousand of the Hegg negatives and hundreds of pictures—my lifetime goal and Mr. Hegg's goal, at last complete.

In Mr. Hegg's generally happy life, there was one sad day I was witness to; that was his last day at his Bellingham studio, before his move to San Diego. He was then seventy-nine. His eyes grew misty in this, his final farewell to his beloved cameras and all his other photographic equipment. The parting was harder than any ascent to Chilkoot. That day he gave me clippings and newspaper articles of his work.

Because of his rare photographic skill and artistry, posterity will forever be able to follow the old Sourdough Trail up the Alaskan Coast, over the Dyea Trail, over Chilkoot, over White Pass, through Canyon City, Sheep Camp, and Log Cabin; and again whipsaw lumber at Lake Bennett, skirt shifting sandbars of the Yukon to Dawson and the gold fields of the Klondike—in a medium we all understand, the universal language of pictures.

Ethel Anderson Becker

*Every story and every picture of pure raw gold sent hundreds of eager men
following the thousands who had gone before.*

1
GOLD!
in the
Klondike . . .

IN JULY 1897, thousands of people in hundreds of American towns heard the clarion call of gold and the roll of golden drums. The Steamer *Excelsior* had arrived in San Francisco harbor out of the Klondike with a cargo of gold. On her decks was a crowd of jubilant prospectors; in her holds, a fortune in the precious metal. Aboard was a farmer who had panned out $130,000; a clerk who had dug up $85,000, and a blacksmith-by-trade who had taken out $115,000.

Two days later, the one-time whaler, *Portland,* docked at Seattle with even greater riches; she carried a ton of Klondike gold, and this was only a sample of what was to come. One man had sluiced out $24,000 in a day; another, $50,000 in a week; and another had washed $800 out of one pan. And this Klondike gold was not just gold dust; it was coarse gold nuggets — even chunks up to the size of a man's fist and more.

With a single convulsion, west coast cities shook off the depression doldrums that had been growing steadily worse since the Panic of 1893. The nation followed suit, and Seattle became the launching pad for every kind of craft that could float. Teachers left their classrooms, farmers their farms, and clerks their stores, in the mad rush for gold—the magic metal that would transform their lives.

THIS IS GEORGE W. CARMACK, *whose discovery of gold on Rabbit Creek eventually started some 200,000 people to the gold fields of the Klondike—more than a fourth of whom arrived. Carmack was born in California, September 24, 1860, the son of a Forty-Niner, and came north on a windjammer in 1885. Landing at Dyea, Alaska, he made his way into the Lake Bennett country, where he met and married a young Tagish Indian woman. Hunting, trading, and fishing with the natives, he had won considerable influence among them when his path crossed that of Bob Henderson.*

THIS IS BOB HENDERSON, *the Canadian prospector who suggested that George Carmack try the gravel on Rabbit Creek. Henderson himself fared but poorly. All the claims had been staked on the creek and its gold-bearing tributaries when news of Carmack's success finally reached his isolated camp at Gold Bottom Creek. Henderson was later pensioned by the Canadian government for his part in the discovery—with it understood that he would prospect no more! He died an embittered man.*

THIS IS PHOTOGRAPHER ERIC A. HEGG *with his outfit moving across Lake Bennett country. When Hegg joined other stampeders to the Klondike in 1897, he was a journeyman photographer with a genius for being in the right place at the right time. In mid-winter he took a sled-load of photographic equipment across the coast range, and under conditions that would have daunted a softer man, he took a series of photographs that have perpetuated the glory and the hardships of the gold-crazed stampeders.*

Behind all the uproar lay a single—almost accidental—discovery. On August 14, 1896, George W. Carmack, veteran hunter and sometime prospector, found color in the gravel bed of Rabbit Creek, a tributary of the Klondike River. Three days later he staked his claim on that creek, which he renamed the Bonanza. On September 24, Carmack registered his "Discovery" claim and a sample of the ore with Captain C. Constantine of the Canadian Northwest Mounted Police, at Forty-Mile. Staking claims at the same time—"one above and one below"—were his Indian in-laws who had been with him at the time of discovery: "Tagish" Charlie and "Skookum" Jim. His handsome Tagish Indian wife Kate was also present.

Though Carmack receives popular credit for the discovery, another man, Bob Henderson, a Canadian ex-sailor turned prospector, gets official credit. As early as 1895, Henderson had picked up gold on Rabbit Creek. He had been grubstaked by Joseph Ladue, operator of a trading post at Forty-mile. The following summer, when Henderson was on his way down the Yukon River for supplies, he met Carmack, who was fishing at the mouth of the Klondike. As was customary in the country, he suggested that Carmack try his luck where he himself had found traces of gold—and he gave the exact location. Carmack took his advice some two weeks later. But—Carmack registered his claim, and Henderson did not!

Carmack had little to say about his discovery, and what he did say got scant heed from the veteran miners of the region, who considered him something of a greenhorn. However, they did listen to the enthusiastic reports of Trading Post Proprietor Joseph Ladue, who gave out glowing accounts to all who stopped at his post. As word got around, more and more prospectors began arriving. A general movement started at Forty-Mile, and another at Circle City.

During the fall of 1896, Carmack did some fair sluicing, but not until November 3, when considerable gold was picked up near the surface of Claim No. 21, above Carmack's, did the real rush start. At No. 21, gravel yielded about $500 to the cubic yard; previous high in the Yukon basin had been only about $10 per cubic yard.

Not until the following July did word get Outside—when the *Portland* and the *Excelsior* sailed into Pacific Coast ports bringing prospectors with the gold yield of their spring sluicing.

By the first of August 1897, over four thousand gold seekers had sailed for the gold fields from Seattle, and twenty-five hundred from Tacoma. Thousands sailed from San Francisco, Portland, Victoria, Vancouver, and other Pacific Coast ports. When passage was sold out, stampeders chartered cattle boats, scows, tugs, and all sorts of smaller craft in a mad race up the Alaskan Coast.

Attached to every westbound train was a "gold rush" car which advertised the Klondike. Glass jars filled with nuggets and gold dust lined the walls, along with photographs of mines, log cabins, creek beds, and piles of dirt. Books and pamphlets describing the Klondike were distributed among the passengers. Gold bricks gleamed in the sunlight.

Meanwhile, information concerning this new bonanza land was scant and scattered. Even the boundary line was not officially determined. In 1889, Canadian Dominion Surveyor William Ogilvie had completed a tentative boundary survey, which was uncontested till after the gold rush started. The boundary between the "panhandle" of Alaska and Canada was then hotly disputed. Skagway and Dyea—gateways to the Klondike—were in the disputed area. The United States claimed the region by right of purchase; Canada, by right of settlement. While thousands joined the wild stampede, two great countries wrestled with the problem of establishing the boundary line. Canadians finally yielded until such time as a tribunal should settle the matter. They constructed their customs offices on the mountain summits above the two towns.

The *Excelsior*, the *Portland*, the *Al-ki*, the *Tampico*, and the *Willamette*, loaded with gold-hungry stampeders, grubstakes, horses, and hay, shuttled up and down the Alaskan Coast, followed by an armada of sailing vessels, launches, fishing boats, and tugs towing top-heavy scows. Unseaworthy boats were manned by crews who

The Steamer Portland *cuts through ice floes in the Gulf of Alaska.*

The gold-laden Excelsior *arrives in San Francisco.*

had never heard of freezing *williwaws*, tide rips, or the churning waters which lashed the rock-strewn coast. Men stormed ticket offices begging passage, offering to pay fabulous prices for tickets already sold. Steamship companies, desperate for this new surge of business, searched the far seas for additional vessels. Men who could not go dipped their fingers into the pot of gold by grubstaking those who could.

After a stormy winter trip up the coast, the Steamer *Al-ki* arrived in Skagway. The vessel belonged on Puget Sound, where the weather was fair and the coastline familiar; but pressed into the emergency, she broke all records for the number of trips made during the gold rush. Horses, mules, and sheep jammed the forward deck. Hay and feed pyramided to the pilot house. Barnyard stench permeated the ship and worried the seasick. Emergency bunks along the decks gave uneasy slumber to some two hundred gold seekers. On arrival in Dyea and Skagway, the bunks and pens were dismantled and the lumber sold for $300 or more per thousand feet.

Alaska's coastline became the graveyard of the world. A staggering number of boats were wrecked during gold-rush days. The year 1898 held the record, averaging three ships a month. In 1906, twenty-five boats failed to reach port. In 1910, Alaskan waters claimed twenty-two more. These disasters were caused by the uncharted seas, inexperienced pilots, long winter nights, fog, wind and rocks.

The Al-ki, after a stormy trip up the coast, arrives in Skagway. She was the first boat to leave Seattle for the Klondike after the arrival of the steamer, Portland, *with her cargo of gold.*

Stampeders learned that the North was not entirely an unknown land. Old Spanish explorers, a century earlier, had pointed the way to the Klondike. And Russian traders had suppressed the knowledge of gold in the Yukon country on penalty of death, because a gold rush would ruin the fur trade. One day *hootchinoo*, foul-tasting bootleg whiskey, backfired and a native talked too much. Over the entire Yukon, the story of his sudden death was hushed from mouth to mouth, but the whisper of gold brought outsiders into the North.

Little by little, letters from these men—prospectors, trappers, and missionaries—seeped out to the home folks of the world. The contagion of these whispers reached others. Very slowly the Great North drew to herself a small race of men who spread out along the tributaries of the mighty Yukon, each hoping some day to make the big strike. All of this, however, was prior to the discovery on Bonanza Creek.

Coastal Indian village with totem poles.

The Alaskan Coast held many curious sights for the stampeders, and one of the strangest was the totem poles. Captain James Cook, the early explorer, and Captain John Meares, the fur trader, had been the first to observe the weird rituals and ceremonies centering around the birds and animals which were interwoven in the natives' religion. Later this was identified as Totemism. Strange figures depicting legends and tribal culture were carved not only on totem poles but on the tools the natives used in their daily life. Iron tools later enabled them to make the elaborate carvings which grew out of their legends and religion. Soon whole forests of totem poles appeared in every village. When the government began its control of Indian affairs and the clergy began to superimpose its beliefs on the Indians' beliefs— "There is but one God"—the culture of carving began to decline and the tribal totem poles fell into the hands of collectors and all but disappeared.

This Congressional Party, which visited Alaska in 1900, was as curious about totem poles as the stampeders had been.

*The great Malaspina Glacier,
between Juneau and Cordova.*

Passengers from the Portland *barter for
Indian relics at Wrangell.*

From shipboard, Alaska seemed a country of sculptured majesty. Stampeders, sprawled atop their baggage, studied the impossible mountain barriers, and in imagination made camp, climbed cliffs, packed food—and planned how to get ahead of their companions. With the gold fever racing through their blood, even the trek over the mountains seemed easy.

Ghost-like glaciers, pushing blue fingers through the sharp ravines to the water's edge, made a formidable barricade. There the ice rested to be carved by storm and tide into overhanging shelves. Bombarded by waves or knifed by steamboat whistles, a ledge would snap, drop, and sink slowly from sight. Like a cumbersome animal, an iceberg would rise, revolve slowly as it sought its equilibrium, and be carried away by the tide. The Malaspina Glacier between Juneau and Cordova, with a Pacific Ocean frontage of sixty miles, is the greatest in the world.

The Thlingit Indians, along Alaska's southeast coast, were noted for their carvings, beadwork and beautiful basketry; but visitors found them moody and difficult to deal with, shrewdly refusing to barter when they did not receive what an article was worth. They would patiently await the arrival of another steamer with other prospects. Suspicious and susceptible to Indian tradition, they would squat at the very edge of the wharf—for it was considered bad luck to allow anyone to pass behind them.

Through the doors of this Russian log trading post at Sitka once passed Indians and trappers with furs enough for a Czar's ransom. Along its weatherbeaten length, native women awaited a buyer for their wares. Thus they have waited for over a hundred years.

From the board walk along the front of the post could be seen the Cathedral of St. Michael (far left), built in 1847-1849. The church, since destroyed by fire, contained priceless paintings and tapestries brought from Russia.

Because it was the capital of Russian America, and the headquarters of the dynamic Russian ruler, Alexander Baranov, Sitka emulated the courts of St. Petersburg in entertainment, but had the added color of natives, totem poles and traders—a strange conglomeration.

The Steamer Colorado, *wrecked during gold-rush days, lies in Wrangell Narrows, where it lent itself to modern advertising: "Drink Clarks Rye & Yellowstone Whiskey."*

16

*Gold seekers, Klondike bound, from the Schwabacker Wharf, Seattle.
The S.S.* Tampico *is at the right.*

*For four years, crowds like
this surged about the docks
seeking passage to Dyea,
Skagway, or St. Michael.*

17

CANYON, DYEA TRAIL.

"*Dyea Canyon opened out finally into a ravine with spreading cliffs;
frozen solid in winter.*"

2

Dyea

and the

Chilkoot Trail

BY FAR THE greater number of stampeders sailed from San Francisco, Seattle, or Vancouver up the inside passage of Southeastern Alaska, to the head of Lynn Canal, landing either on the shores of Dyea Inlet, or near the mouth of the Skagway River. Dyea and Skagway were less than half a dozen miles apart. One trail ran up the canyon of Skagway River to White Pass; the other followed the gorge beyond Dyea to Chilkoot Pass. At first, Chilkoot was the favorite route, and the beach at Dyea received the first hordes of stampeders and their welter of cargo.

Unloading thousands of stampeders and their freight on a long beach was a job of difficulty and confusion. There were no docks, no wharves, and there was no orthodox way of disembarking. The passengers were literally dumped into the sea at the end of Lynn Canal. Many an outfit piled on the sand was lost in the incoming tide. Horses

were swung out over the sea, and dropped into the water to swim ashore. Lighters, previously arranged for by the steamship companies, angled a clumsy course alongside the ships. They were loaded, floated ashore with a racing tide, and beached high and dry by the same tide receding. Provisions were strewn along the cove in wildest disorder—cases of evaporated milk, dried fruit, beans, rice, flour, and bacon. Defying segregation, lumber, sleds, boats, knock-down steamers, picks and shovels, gold pans, and all manner of mining contraptions deluged a once quiet landscape.

Everywhere was disregard for weaklings; everywhere, bewilderment. And everywhere a wild eagerness to "hurry, hurry" prevailed. The first arrivals found nothing that smacked of civilization, nothing but a treacherous tide and mud flats behind, and glowering, dark mountains ahead. And it was beyond those mountains that

It was often a rush against both time and tide to get freight above the high-water line ahead of the incoming tide. Canny teamsters charged more than twice the fee when the tide was rising than when it was falling—and few stampeders wanted to waste precious time arguing.

Trail Street, Dyea, 1898.

the gold lay—six hundred miles distant. The important thing was to hurry, to get there before the world poured in its thousands. There was no time to sleep now, no time to eat. It was thirty-five miles through a mountain pass to Lake Bennett. They must hurry, hurry, before King Winter locked the Yukon under six feet of ice.

In a year's time, Dyea had begun to take on the semblance of a city. Cooks opened restaurants and coffee tents. Real estate men began pyramiding property values. The need for a doctor transformed one man's tent into an operating room, and he never found time to complete his dash to the gold fields. Aching teeth anchored a dentist. Engineers studied the trail with its packing tortures, and the aerial tramway was born. Thus began the gold seekers' rehabilitation in the Great North.

Prior to the gold rush, the only white-man resident in Dyea had been Sam Heron, who operated the Healy and Wilson Trading Post. Then it had been an important occasion when some prospector or trader stopped to buy supplies on his way over Chilkoot Pass. The Indians of Lynn Canal worked in the fish cannery at Chilkat, or fished for salmon along the coast. For the most part, living was serene. Now overnight the cannery was idle, lacking laborers. This yellow metal in the earth had brought an exciting new world to their unruffled existence.

Nine miles from Dyea, in the shelter of the stone walls of Dyea Canyon, stampeders set up their tents as they relayed their outfits. Here Canyon City grew to a camp of more than three thousand inhabitants. Through this canyon were hauled boats and knock-down mills. Tenderfeet pushed wheelbarrows and pulled frail two-wheel carts. A pack train of ten horses earned at least $100 a day and a wagon and team $25—a cost prohibitive to the great majority of gold seekers. Native packers arrogantly went on strike.

While stampeders worried about transporting their outfits, the Indians sat stolidly by, counting the money from the last job and watching—with eyes that fairly bugged—the strange sights which had dissipated the monotony in their domain. The trails soon choked with freight while prices for packing rose ever higher. Few could afford the quick increases. Harder work, longer hours, heavier loads, less sleep, and less food fell to the lot of the stampeders.

Dyea Canyon opened out finally into a ravine with spreading cliffs; frozen solid in winter. Spring brought a succession of sump holes, bogs, and mountain cascades roaring full of ice water. Floundering pack horses blockaded the trail.

Fall rains and the feet of men and women churned the trail into a bottomless mire. Mules, oxen, and pack trains, top-heavy with boxes and sacks, stumbled along, flogged on by desperate teamsters until they floundered in the sea of mud. The animals lay where they fell, starved, weak, and broken-limbed. The stench of bloated fly-blown carcasses filled the air and polluted the streams where stampeders paused to drink.

Bitter rivalry grew up between Skagway and Dyea as businessmen of each city tried to draw business by keeping the trail in good repair.

Nine miles from Dyea, in the shelter of the stone walls of Dyea Canyon.

With his pack for a pillow, an exhausted '98 stampeder sinks down beside the trail.

"Grub snatching" was not uncommon. When caught, the thief was tried by his own trail fellows. Punishment was swift and sure.

The conscience of one "grub snatcher" meted out his penalty down through thirty long years. His own outfit had been lost in the quick, racing tide at Dyea. Gone now was the mortgaged home in Oregon. Gone was the hope of Klondike gold. As he watched others pass him by, crazy ideas surged over him. Then one day he came on a cache just off the beaten path. He decided to move it. Beneath the canvas cover he found the owner, drugged by sleep and weariness. Startled and thwarted, he grabbed the pick and crushed the sleeper. He dug a hole in the sand and rolled the body into it. All but the hand. A hurried, deeper excavation followed—still the hand. Three times he dug. But always when he returned for another pack, the hand was reaching out to him.

The "grub snatcher" amassed a fortune and returned to the "outside" where he took his prosperous place among men. All the good things he enjoyed he owed to the grubstake he had stolen that long-ago day; yet always he could see the hand reaching out. He finally confessed. But the hand still beckoned and he followed it through an open door—the insane asylum. There, some said, in the still of the night, his anguished cry would often ring out, "The hand! The hand!"

The Northwest Mounted Police prepare to meet the horde of stampeders.

With the first announcement of the discovery of gold on Bonanza Creek, the Canadian Government, ever watchful of the possibilities of disorder within its borders, prepared to meet the hordes rushing toward the gold fields. Setting up headquarters for the Northwest Mounted Police on the summits of Chilkoot and the White Pass trails, they tried to weed out the tinhorn gamblers and undesirables, and accept only substantial, hard-working men.

As early as 1869, Hudson's Bay Company men had found the first traces of gold along the Yukon River, and this became a magnet to prospectors all over the world. As the scattered population increased, need for some sort of policing became necessary. In 1894, a detachment of twenty Northwest Mounted Police was sent to the Dawson country under command of Captain C. Constantine. There they established themselves at Forty-Mile. Next an officer was sent to take charge of the customs. Still later, a gold commissioner was appointed. It was at Forty-Mile that George Carmack registered his claim in 1896.

Because there was no precedent to follow, the first months of 1897 were filled with wild disorder. That same year, twenty more police were added to the force. In the early part of the rush, stampeders were allowed to enter Canada regardless of the size of their food supply. Later, when starvation threatened, a minimum of twelve hundred pounds per person was required to enter into Canadian territory.

The number of Mounted Police increased with the population, until in 1900 the force included three hundred men. Klondike gold had brought stampeders swarming down the Mackenzie River and up the Yukon; up the Fraser and through the Caribou; over the Edmonton Trail and over the Dalton Trail. Through Canada's every door hurried thousands to dip first fingers into the pot of gold.

Crime, however, never has been prevalent in the Yukon, and there have been remarkably few hold-ups. Besides, one never argues with the Royal Mounted Police. One of their chief duties was to stop the sale of liquor to the Indians; another was to provide medical care, medicine, and food for the sick and destitute.

Sheep Camp.

Sheep Camp, twelve miles from Dyea, offered a natural setting for a campsite, and the valley soon became a city of close to eight thousand gold seekers. Telegraph lines were established early in the gold rush, but maintenance was difficult because of the winds and snowstorms.

Many years previous to the gold rush, hunters for mountain sheep had established their quarters in this wind-swept valley, causing it to be known as Sheep Camp. The sparsely forested foothills furnished the last fuel on the western side of the divide.

Here in this tent city the Australians made dampers, the Scotsmen made flannel cakes, the Americans made flapjacks, and from them all the Great North made sourdough hot cakes.

It was to Sheep Camp that victims of the April 1898 snowslide were taken for identification. The Northwest Mounted Police, stationed at the tentative boundary line, hurried over and gave assistance.

Heavy packs and cramped muscles, galling packstraps, sweat smarting the sore places, heavy boots, and broken blisters—such was the Klondike Trail. When the Canadian authorities decreed that each stampeder must bring enough supplies for a year, not many could afford the luxury of hiring the Chilkat Indian bearers, who soon learned the art of bargaining. Most of the time the stampeders simply shuttled back and forth with their supplies, every man strictly for himself.

Here is a close-up view of the last climb to the summit of Chilkoot. The charge varied from five cents per pound to thirty-five cents, according to the season and type of load. The dark streaks to the right of the packers are the trails made by stampeders on their wild slide to the base of the mountain to get another load.

Approaching the summit of Chilkoot.

Summit of Chilkoot Pass, showing The Scales, a little valley that was the last staging area before the stampeders went "over the top." Here men rounded up their packs and prepared for the final assault on the mountain: a grade of thirty degrees up some twelve hundred steps gouged into frozen snow. The Scales got its name from the Indian guides who weighed their packs here on a primitive balance before starting up.

The summit of Chilkoot Pass—four miles beyond Sheep Camp and nearly thirty-six hundred feet above sea level—was windswept and bathed in almost perpetual fog. During the first winter, stampeders climbed the icy slope by crawling up and digging in. Later, Dyea business men chipped steps in the ice and fastened a rope beside the trail for support. Some steps were extended so that a climber could step out of line and rest. The average stampeder made the climb in perhaps an hour, carrying a pack weighing from fifty to a hundred and fifty pounds. Professional packers averaged a hundred pounds. An Indian once lugged a three-hundred-and-fifty pound barrel, and a raw-boned Swede crawled up the icy slope on his hands and knees, with three long four-by-six timbers strapped on his back. Summer stampeders found Chilkoot a bouldered mass of rock well nigh impassable.

Having reached the summit, the packer started making his cache by placing a long marker beside his outfit; before he returned, several feet of snow might have covered his precious belongings.

For two years an unending line of men struggled through the coast-range mountain passes, from Dyea to Lake Bennett—a distance of twenty-nine miles. With the completion of the White Pass Railway, the Dyea Trail fell into disuse and Dyea became a ghost town. According to customhouse records at the American-Canadian boundary, more than fifty thousand men passed over the Dyea Trail in two years' time.

To the right of Chilkoot Trail is the Petterson Trail, longer but not so steep and used by pack horses and dog teams. In this picture, markers at the base of the mountain indicate where stampeders have cached their outfits beside tents almost buried by snow. In 1897 a tramline was installed, operated by steam. The tramline can be seen to the left.

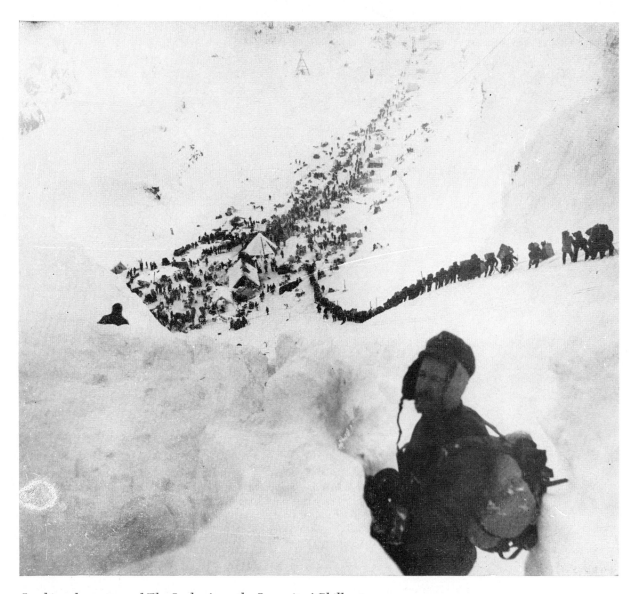

Looking down toward The Scales from the Summit of Chilkoot.

The way down for a new load was easier and faster than the way up. Some walked but many rode down on a shovel, or slid on the seat of their pants.

To the left in this picture is a stampeder preparing to return by way of the "grease trail." There was no stopping or turning back once the wild descent was begun. In the foreground a stampeder looks into the camera before starting down a lane cut shoulder deep in the snow. Hegg got some of his best shots from the dizzy heights of Chilkoot Pass.

One of the first and most famous of the chee-chakos over the Chilkoot Trail was Joaquin Miller, the Poet of the Sierras. In 1897 he was sent north by William Randolph Hearst of the San Francisco *Examiner* to give the people back home a graphic, on-the-spot account of the gold fields — along with whatever poetic furbelows Miller chose to adorn it. One of the stories the poet told about himself was that, while lost in a blizzard, one of his toes was frozen off. He joked about it around the campfire: "I'm the most no-toe-rious poet in America."

Hardships and suffering were common on the trail, but only one major disaster was recorded—the great avalanche on Chilkoot Pass the morning of April 3, 1898.

The winter of 1897-1898 had been severe, and fierce late-spring storms had added tons of fresh wet snow to the already heavy pack on the summit of the mountain.

After the weather had moderated, stampeders were advised to sleep during the day and do their packing at night when the trail was frozen and safe. Those who ignored the advice—sixty-eight of them—were buried in a massive snow slide that piled wet snow thirty-five feet deep over an area of approximately ten acres. Seven victims were taken out alive, and, of these, three died from injuries. Within an hour after the slide, hundreds of men were on the spot digging out the entombed stampeders. Said one who was rescued, "I thought of home, friends, every act of my life. I was held tight as in a plaster cast. Near me people were groaning, praying. Then I became unconscious. When I awoke, I was on the floor of the powerhouse, alive but black and blue and bruised. They tell me I was buried three hours."

Among those who rushed to the scene was E. A. Hegg, who locked up his studio at Dyea and headed for the pass.

In the spring the mountains echoed with a continuous rumble of avalanches and snow slides. It was a haunting, fearful sound which made some men turn their backs on Klondike gold.

Digging out of a snow slide on Chilkoot Pass, April 1898.

This photograph of a snowstorm on the summit of Chilkoot is considered a most difficult piece of photography. To the right the Canadian flag flies above the customhouse. Temperatures as much as fifty degrees below zero, and the everlasting freezing gales which sweep across the icy pastures, sent numerous gold seekers back to Dyea and home. Many of them, stumbling along, dropped hopelessly beside the way to rest—or freeze. And no one cared. There was something almost barbaric about that gold-rush invasion: humanity and love were submerged in the primal instincts of greed and self-preservation.

Tons of freight were cached on the summit of Chilkoot Pass, but they represented only a part of what had been planned. Many Klondikers, on arriving at The Scales, had given up and returned to Dyea and home, after sizing up that final, near-vertical climb to the top. Yet, according to reports at the Canadian customhouse, more than fifty thousand stampeders were checked through to the interior.

Tons of freight separated by narrow paths were cached on Chilkoot's summit, giving it the appearance of a miniature city. With the slash of a sword across a snowbank, the approximate boundary line between Alaska and Canada had been established and a block customhouse built. By 1898, rules for entry had been made. Every stampeder paid a duty according to his importation. He was required to give an account of himself as well as prove he had sufficient supplies to last at least a year. For his own safety while on Canadian soil, he was required to register at regular, established posts. This registry showed his arrival, time of departure, and his destination. Should he fail to register at the next post in a certain length of time, a Northwest Mounted Police officer would investigate. This insured help in case of accident and it served as a means of catching criminals. The Mounted Police could lay their hands on any wanted person in their territory in a few days.

Once the stampeders had crossed the summit, the trail to the gold fields of the Klondike and Dawson was mostly downhill. A well-beaten route led to Crater Lake, where a saloon offered opportunity to relax with a feeling that the worst of the trip was over.

Freight at the Canadian base of Chilkoot.

Here was the freightyard on the edge of Crater Lake, at the Canadian base of Chilkoot. Sleds skidded across a slope corrugated by blizzards and sun-polished into belts of glassy ice so slick no boot could gouge a foothold. Descending the Canadian slope with their supplies was as difficult a procedure as the climbing had been.

Note that again tents and caches are all but buried with snow. Several pack horses stand unprotected in the cold. When the entire outfit has been packed down from the summit, the stampeder begins the next relay across the frozen surface of Crater Lake, whose shoreline blends with the encircling mountains in the distance.

Looking up the Chilkoot summit from Crater Lake, April 11, 1899. The summit and aerial tramway are silhouetted in moonlight.

"Mushers" tugging loaded sleds across frozen Crater Lake.

Stampeders are on their way, pulling their sleds across the frozen surface of Crater Lake. Sails fashioned from blankets and canvas caught the winds sweeping down from the passes and quickened their speed. Throwing a rope harness over his shoulders, the "musher" tugged his sled loaded with about two hundred pounds of supplies along the winding trail. Sweating, panting, swearing, he advanced a few miles, deposited his load at the new cache, and returned for another. Usually gold seekers worked in parties of two or more, leaving one member to stand guard and cook.

Eric Hegg secured a team of goats to freight supplies across Crater Lake. A large canvas streamer on his sled announced: "Have you seen these views of Alaska? Photographs sent to all parts of the world. E. A. Hegg." The goats were tame animals from Oregon, and they did a creditable job of hauling. When their usefulness was over, they were fattened on the lush green growth along the streams and then slaughtered for food. (See photo on page 10.)

Beyond Crater Lake lay Lake Lindeman, where stampeders prepared for the last leg of their journey to the Klondike.

Lake Lindeman.

Lake Lindeman, at the head of navigation, became a canvas city of five thousand stampeders arriving and leaving continuously. Enterprising real-estate men bought up the level land around Lake Bennett and Lake Lindeman. When the Mounted Police learned that promoters planned to charge each stampeder two dollars for the privilege of setting up his tent, they were expelled from the country. Once settled beside the lake, gold seekers whipsawed lumber in the sparse forests and began to build boats which would carry them through a series of lakes and rivers to the Yukon, Dawson, and the gold fields.

It was on a scaffold such as pictured here that stampeders whipsawed logs into lumber. The tree was felled from a fast-receding forest. After the limbs were trimmed, the log was hoisted to the frame over a pit. The flip of a charcoal-covered string fastened at each end of the log marked the line for the saw to follow. One man pulled the saw up and his partner pulled it down in a shower of sawdust. These mills were called "arm-strong" mills; they worked very efficiently as long as tempers did not grow too short.

Whipsawing logs into lumber.

Looking up White Pass summit from Half Mile below, March 20, 1899.

3

Skagway

and the

White Pass

A N ALTERNATE route to the Klondike lay over White Pass, longer but lower than the Chilkoot route. Its highest elevation was only twenty-nine hundred feet compared to Chilkoot's thirty-five hundred. Despite greater difficulties of travel—particularly the snow-melt that turned it into a veritable bog—the White Pass became the more popular way to Dawson.

On July 26, 1897, the first stampeders landed on the mud flats of present Skagway and swarmed across the old Moore homestead which lay on either side of the Skagway River. The Moore homestead soon became an unorganized city seething with several thousand poachers. Overnight, businessmen took root and not one of them stopped to inquire about rights and ownership of land. Thus was Skagway born.

On August 12, less than one month after the first boat landed, a city organization of a sort was begun, with A. J. McKenny as mayor.

Squatters were ordered to move on. The ugly stockades, which crawled with wild-eyed, mangy cayuses, were torn down. Skagway was then laid out in orderly fashion and soon spread from one mountainside to the other.

Skagway was governed by a group of efficient city fathers. More than a thousand lots sold immediately. Saloons, some sixty-seven of them, hotels, stores, and restaurants were bought, sold, and resold, in a skyrocketing real estate boom.

The "fly-by-night" stampede city was assured long life when Michael Heney, as contractor, Dr. F. B. Whiting, as chief surgeon, E. C. Hawkins, as chief engineer, and P. J. O'Brien, as bridge constructor, arrived and began to recruit construction workers to build the White Pass Railroad. Down-and-outers were glad for the opportunity to earn money to take them on into the gold fields or back home.

The mud flats at Skagway, July 1897. That winter Eric Hegg moved his studio to this prospering town, where "Irish Prince" Mike Heney and "bad man" Jefferson R. Smith were to make history. The wharves shown here helped give Skagway the edge over Dyea because they made it possible for ships to discharge cargo at Skagway rather than offshore.

The Steamer Resolute, tied on the wharf at Skagway, March 10, 1900. Not even the horrors of a northern winter could stop the wild stampede. The Resolute towed scows top-heavy with freight up the wind-lashed coast.

Right: This was Skagway when "Soapy" Smith began his rule of crime.

Below: "Soapy" Smith and his gang.

"Soapy" Smith, the fourth man from the right in this picture, was a thirty-eight-year-old gambler who came originally from Colorado, where he had drifted from one mining camp to another in the business of swindling miners. His real name was Jefferson Randolph Smith, but he was nicknamed "Soapy" when he began selling soap on street corners for one dollar a bar, wrapping a five-dollar bill around one soap bar as a reward to some lucky buyer. Arriving in Skagway with an army of thugs, tinhorn gamblers, shell-game operators, and disreputable women, he began a rule of crime which so alarmed the people of the North that they began to avoid passing through Skagway. Clever in planning crimes for his gang, "Soapy" never personally took part in carrying them out.

When Big Mike, a tough, two-fisted miner, came out from the Klondike, with two pokes of gold dust and nuggets carelessly slung over his shoulder, the gang was on hand. They slugged him and stole the gold. One hour later Big Mike was tearing up the town, storming through Clancy's saloon, and demanding that "Soapy" and his outlaws be run out of town—out of Alaska.

Holly Street, Skagway.

Badge of "Soapy's" army.

This is Holly Street, where in June 1898 "Soapy" Smith drilled his followers, militia-like, through the main streets while all Skagway wondered, "What next?" Pack trains were led aside to let the "army" pass. Stampeders, bent double under heavy loads, stepped back, choking in the dust. Citizens locked their windows, hid their valuables, and planted a loaded gun within easy reach as the rumor spread that "Soapy" was about to take over the town.

"Soapy" Smith drilled his army to military perfection. At the outbreak of the Spanish-American War, he had the nerve to offer President McKinley the services of his Alaska regiment— with himself as commanding officer. At the time, even by the most generous standards, his conduct could have earned him life imprisonment. The offer was refused, but "Captain" Jefferson Smith, as he now called himself, was gradually gaining some recognition in Washington, D. C.

When Skagway planned a celebration for the Fourth of July, which included a parade, "Soapy" dressed his recruits in sailor suits. In appearance, at least, they were presentable. Shown here is a facsimile of the badge which each member of "Soapy's" army wore in that famous Fourth of July parade.

There was an honor guard for Frank Reid, but none for "Soapy." "Soapy's" three ringleaders were afterwards tried in Federal court and given heavy sentences in the penitentiary; the rest of the gang was sent to the States with a warning never to return.

The body of Frank Reid, the man who killed "Soapy" Smith, lies in state under military guard. A one-time school teacher, Reid came from Minnesota to Oregon, and served through the entire campaign of the Piute Indian War. Later he worked with a surveying crew in New Whatcom (now Bellingham), Washington. In 1897, he joined the gold rush and soon became civil engineer for Skagway. Frank Reid was a crack shot with a rifle and a stickler for what he thought was right.

In July 1898, a vigilante group of outraged citizens was organized; Frank Reid was among them. The group met at the city hall to devise some method of ridding Skagway of this one-man directed crime wave. Because of the need for greater secrecy, the vigilantes adjourned to the warehouse at the end of Sylvester Dock. It was at the approach to this dock that Frank Reid

challenged "Soapy" Smith. When "Soapy" refused to halt at Mr. Reid's command, both men exchanged shots. "Soapy" died immediately. Reid lingered for a time.

Other leaders of the outlaw gang were immediately captured and sentenced. Followers fled and Skagway settled back to new freedom. A granite column in the cemetery at Skagway bears the inscription, *"Frank Reid. Died July 20, 1898. Age 54 years. He gave his life for the honor of Skagway."* Not far away a weather-beaten board reads, *"Jefferson R. Smith. Died July 8, 1898. Age 38 years."*

History frequently casts a tolerant eye on the villain—especially one as colorful as "Soapy." Today in Skagway the reconstructed "Jeff Smith's Parlor" is one of the most popular tourist attractions.

E. A. Hegg's studio in Skagway.

Photographer Hegg's first studio in Dyea was built out of lumber from dismantled dories. Inside this shack that leaked both water and light, he set up a small tent as a dark room for developing pictures. Later he moved to Skagway where his modern studio was an attraction for all who passed. Stampeders and reporters supplied themselves with pictures which showed the immensity of the gold rush far better than words—and incidentally kept the mad migration surging on.

Ben Atwater, the man in the sled, and his famous team of hounds carried mail from Skagway to Nome, a distance of twenty-three hundred miles. This dog team held an unbroken record for speed. In his younger days, Atwater was known as the "strong man of America." He came to Alaska in 1865 and spent sixty years as one of the Northland's most outstanding pioneers. He passed away in Anchorage at the age of eighty-five.

Two missionaries, the Reverends Dickey and Grant—at the extreme left and extreme right in the picture—arrived at Skagway in January 1898. Packing like any stampeder on the White Pass Trail, they earned warm places in the hearts of their fellow travelers.

Klondike bound.

Klondike-bound and led by a piper, a party prepares to leave Skagway for the White Pass Trail. Stampeders brought a great assortment of dogs to the gold rush, many of which were stolen from the streets of Seattle. In the snow fields they led a "dog's life."

Any dog that could "pull" was harnessed. Rails came later, but for the first two years, dogs and horses, stampeders and Chilkat Indians packed the freight to Dawson.

The Klondike gold rush had also caused great excitement in England, Ireland, and Scotland. In 1899, Alex McDonald, who later became known as the King of the Klondike, formed a company in London called McDonald's Bonanza, Ltd., with a capital of 450,000 shares—115,000 preferred and 335,000 common. The preferred shares were entitled to one hundred per cent dividends before ordinary shares could participate.

English Royalty bowed low to the golden idol of the Klondike. In 1898, the Duke of Fife, son-in-law of the Prince of Wales, subscribed to an enterprise known as the Klondyke Exploration Company, Ltd. But while legitimate mining companies were being organized world-wide, many fake mining corporations were also drawing tens of thousands of dollars from the pockets of the citizenry.

A wagon road through the cut-off, three and a half miles from the summit of White Pass. Note the abandoned equipment and goods cached beside the trail.

Pack train in Box Canyon, on White Pass Trail.

Famous "Dead Horse Gulch" led from Skagway to the summit of White Pass. It was a crude Indian path that natives had used on their trips from the coast to the interior during their annual moose-hunting quests. As thousands of men and animals floundered over it, in many places it became a quagmire of knee-deep mud. At other places, sharp rocks had become exposed and reached out, dagger-like, to cut both man and beast.

This pack train was traveling through Box Canyon, March 30, 1899. Unless carefully packed, the corners of the loads gouged sores in the backs of the pack animals. The life of each horse averaged six weeks. Horses that stumbled and fell were lashed up by cursing teamsters—only to fall again. Animals screamed in the cold and refused to jump until drivers themselves led the way. Blizzards raged through the long winter. Ice covered everything, and when it snowed the trail was lost.

The story of the Klondike pack horse is filled with unparalleled cruelty. Not the wildest imagination could picture the reality of the early White Pass Trail. Many men joining the gold rush hoped for fortunes in working pack trains, and the demand for horse flesh was so great in Seattle that horse markets were filled with broncos from the plains, old nags from the farm, and mules and oxen from the logging camps. Before the main force of the rush began, drivers could take their time in packing. Later, some teamsters crowded and forced their animals. Food was scarce and expensive. It was easier to feed oats than to bother with hay. Horses weakened, stumbled, and died. Thousands lay where they fell, their bodies and their bones forming part of the trail.

Men who ran pack trains, though, generally tried to handle their animals sensibly, watering them with warm water, feeding them sufficiently, and blanketing them at night. Because the pack train was their fortune, these men learned to load the animals skillfully to prevent the pack from rubbing sores in their backs.

Winter layered the ravines with snow and froz-

en carcasses. Summer brought the stench from rotting horseflesh sweeping through the trails, borne by the everlasting gales into Skagway. With the stench came blowflies, enormous ugly creatures that covered everything in a black shroud. They swarmed into tents and crawled over food and dishes. Businessmen from Skagway, working madly to meet the increasing surge of trail business, realized the threat to their health. They hurried up the White Pass Trail, cleared away the debris, widened the trail, and burned the putrid horseflesh and blowflies. For a few miles, temporarily at least, the situation was bettered.

"The story of the Klondike pack horse is filled with unparalleled cruelty."

A mule collapses on the White Pass Trail.

Joe Brooks' pack train is held up on the trail between Log Cabin and Lake Bennett by the collapse of one of the mules. Good pack animals were in great demand, for in the early days of the gold rush one pound of food was considered equal to a pound of gold.

This is the famous "Bottle House" at the summit of White Pass. The quantity of bottles indicates their extensive use in the Klondike stampede. The roof of this house followed the customary roof pattern in Alaska—small poles laid close together and covered with moss and canvas. Over the canvas was spread a layer of dirt.

Bottles also made excellent candle holders, and they fitted suitably into such other improvised table equipment as tin-can bread holders. Ingenious gold rushers made excellent glasses out of them as well, after removing the necks of the bottles. This was neatly done by means of a twine dipped in coal oil and wrapped tightly around the bottle. The twine was touched with a lighted match and burned. The bottle was then quickly immersed in cold water, the contraction causing the glass to crack evenly where the twine was wrapped.

"Bottle House" at the summit of the Pass.

Two stampeders haul fourteen hundred pounds with one horse over the summit of White Pass. The winter trail was clean and safe compared to the summer trail, but at no time was there feed in the mountain canyons—and in winter there was no water. When hay was gone, drivers lashed pack animals as long as they could stand, forcing them on. When the animals became too weak to walk, they were turned loose among the barren rocks to die, unless shot out of their misery by some humane stampeder.

Sleds become two-wheeled carts.

All manner of conveyances to carry supplies appeared along the trail. These particular stampeders on the White Pass Trail solved their transportation problem by putting wooden wheels, sawed from the butt of a tree, under their sleds.

Some built two-wheeled carts. Others made wagons of Peterborough canoes—an all-wood craft very popular in Canada. They hoped these amphibious vehicles would later hasten their speed to Dawson.

The building of White Pass Railway begins as gangs of workmen blast a right-of-way into sheer rock walls that shoulder out the sky. The muffled rumble of the huge blasts punctuates the northern stillness like the sound of heavy artillery.

Contractor Michael J. Heney, an Irish-Canadian thirty-five years of age, had been a railroad builder in the United States but he had never tackled a tough mountain pass before. It intrigued him to tackle the building of a railroad that James Hill, the veteran American railroad builder, said could not be built. After making a survey of the country, alone and unaided financially, he convinced Sir Thomas Tancrede, a London engineer of international repute; Mr. S. H. Graves, an American representative; and Mr. E. C. Hawkins, a railroad builder from Seattle, that by switchbacks and tunneling it was possible.

The Close Brothers of England, through Sir Tancrede, decided to finance the work.

The gold rush was at its height when the building of the White Pass Railway began; August 1, 1898, found workers blasting the stern mountain-side for the laying of the track. Just below in this photograph can be seen the wagon road which business men of Skagway built for the stampeders. Far below, in the bottom of the ravine, the old Moore Trail used by the early argonauts lies abandoned.

This "wild cat" railway, as doubting citizens called it, was unwelcome to many. Gambling dens, saloons and dance halls were reaping a rich harvest when, because of impassable trails, incoming travelers were detained in Skagway. Outfitting companies and the hotels did a thriving business. Packers with good pack trains built fortunes transporting supplies over the White Pass Trail. In spite of difficulties, construction on the railway advanced mile by mile, bridging ravines and slicing the mountains. Each section of railway was put in use as soon as completed.

The winding White Pass Trail can be seen cutting through White Pass City.

While the track was being laid, great snow slides would come hurling down the mountain sides, burying the track under many feet of snow. Sometimes trees would be torn from the mountain and cast directly across the path of the workmen.

By March 30, 1899, the right-of-way cut a straight line along a high level of the mountains. About two thousand workers were scattered along the grade. The winter had been long and hard. Arctic blizzards whined continuously and blanched men's ears and noses a funereal white. Far below they could see the gold seekers on the way to easy gold . . . then, suddenly, without warning, workers threw down their tools, drew their pay, and followed the gold seekers, while other down-and-outers took over the construction job.

Here supplies are being sledded up the winter trail of White Pass on March 24, 1899, for use by the builders of the White Pass Railway. For days at a time, blizzards and storms made freighting impossible. With clear weather the mighty cavalcade moved on to the various places where right-of-way work had begun. As soon as the right-of-way for the railroad was slashed, stampeders and pack trains began to use the easier route.

A quarter of a mile from the boundary line between Alaska and Canada, the pack trains were unloaded—everything except the blankets. Few knew that the blankets were purposely left on the horses to cover any sores on their backs; the Mounted Police would shoot on sight any such animals crossing into Canadian territory. Mingling with packers along this route, a lone woman dragged her sled, heavily loaded with a laundry outfit. "I'm going to clean up Dawson," she said. And she did. Here also came a mother with her babe in arms.

Joe Brooks' mule team is packing crated turkeys to Lake Bennett, where they will be shipped down the Yukon to Dawson, so Klondike millionaires will have a Christmas feast.

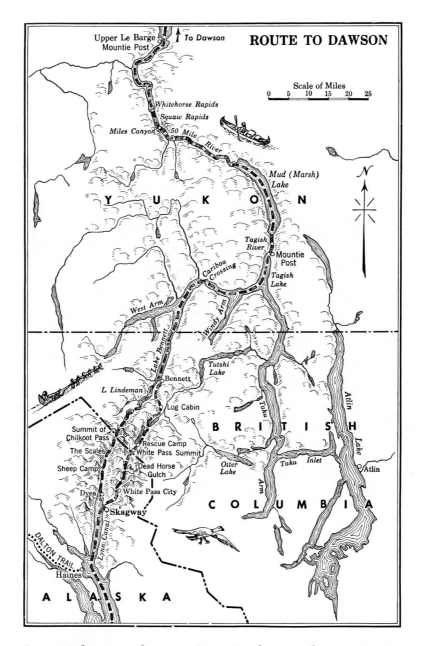

Route of the stampeders from Lynn Canal, across the summits of Chilkoot and White Pass and on to Dawson.

Lake Bennett at the head of navigation offered a water route through lakes and rivers to Dawson, 550 miles away. Summer breezes, fragrant with earthy smells, fragrant too, with forget-me-nots, roses, buttercups, and acres of fireweed, dispelled forever the notion that the Great North was a land of perpetual snow. Even the mountains, at times as stern and unrelenting as pyramids, glowed with a rose-tinted radiance. Before rails ever reached here, a town had mushroomed on the shores of the lake.

4

Lake Bennett

Where

Trails Meet

IN 1898, the settlement at Lake Bennett boasted ten thousand stampeders, the largest tent city and the greatest boatbuilding center in the world. It echoed with the whine of saws, the crashing of trees, the blows of axes, and the tap of caulking irons as men who had never hammered a nail or sawed a board—and they were legion—set about building scows, dories, and rowboats, each according to his own fancy.

Ice was drifting in Lake Bennett when a nineteen-year-old lad arrived and announced he had come all the way from Dawson, rowing across the lakes and dragging his boat upriver to White Horse. From there he had followed the shoreline. His pack, which he said held "grub," actually contained eighty-five pounds of gold dust and nuggets as big as one's thumb. It had been a long torturous journey, that five hundred and fifty miles of fighting Yukon currents. He had thrown his pack away several times; even gold had not seemed worth that much struggle. But always he had returned, shouldered the pack again, and gone on. The end of his journey was near. Skagway was less than fifty miles away.

Winter in Bennett City, on the shores of the lake.

Winter travel along the streets of Bennett City, which grew into a substantial settlement, was spurred on by the thousands of stampeders who stopped temporarily on their rush to the Klondike. By 1898, a few steamers conducted regular runs across the lake, making connections with river boats on the Yukon. The Moran shipyards in Seattle, sensing the great need for sternwheelers, laid the keels of twelve boats in one day. Bennett City, with its stores, hotels, saloons, and dance halls, was a magnet for the workers of the White Pass Railway.

On July 6, 1899, aristocracy and royalty from an entire world boarded the excursion train at Skagway to make the first trip over the completed forty miles of the White Pass Railway to Lake Bennett. It was a gala day. The engine was draped on one side with the American flag, on the other with the Canadian flag. At Bennett, social-ites in a dazzling array of perfumed finery mingled with Yukon mushers, Indians, and roughly dressed railway workers. Financiers from England proudly surveyed the project into which they had poured their millions, all the while projecting themselves into the opportunities which this new land presented. With speeches and great ceremony, the last spike was finally driven to connect the track begun at Skagway with the track begun at White Horse.

The first passenger train to leave Lake Bennett on the White Pass Railway carried $500,000 in gold dust. For contractor Michael Heney it was a job well done. The link connecting the outside world with the Yukon had been forged and financial backers were pleased. Men with pioneer vision saw in this great project the lasting importance and the potential wealth of the North. This gold rush was more than a gold rush. It was the conquest of a last frontier.

Driving the last spike on the White Pass & Yukon Railroad at Lake Bennett.

The first passenger train leaves Lake Bennett. Note the informal flat-bed accommodations.

Ben Atwater, mail carrier, arrives at the Klondike Hotel, Lake Bennett, on his midwinter trip to Skagway. On his sled, wrapped in waterproof canvas, are hundreds of letters from Dawson. No outside mail arrived in the Klondike from September 1898 until January 1899. March brought a heavy mail sack containing over 5,700 registered letters alone. Sometimes as many as fifteen hundred men would wait in line for their mail, regardless of the weather. In June 1899, a money-order branch was established and during the four years following a total of $4,250,000 in money orders was issued.

Mail carrier, Ben Atwater, and his reliable dog team.

The Y. M. C. A., Salvation Army, and various churches made their influence felt from the beginning of the gold rush. In August of 1899, the Y. M. C. A. chartered the *Clifford Sifton* for an excursion around Lake Bennett.

The Clifford Sifton, *an excursion boat on Lake Bennett.*

These outfits are bound for the gold fields, along the frozen course of the Yukon. When financially able, stampeders like these freighted their outfits by horse team along the banks of the Yukon. Note the number of boats caught in the freeze-up of the river. The following summer, boat builders salvaged the wrecks, burned the boats, and picked the nails out of the ashes to construct other boats.

Many stampeders did not wait for the spring break-up, but headed out over the frozen wastes, bold and desperate in their greed to be among the first in the gold fields.

Ice motors leave Bennett for Dawson on March 16, 1899. The motorized sled was guided by means of a disc controlled by a steering wheel, with a bar attachment to give greater leverage. Since little is known about this mode of travel, it is assumed it was not very effective.

It was safer and made for greater speed for stampeders to band together—like those shown here—when headed for gold across the frozen surface of Lake Bennett.

The canvas bag on the front of the sled in the foreground is labeled "E. T. Dailey." Close observation will reveal the efficiency of this outfit:

Klondike-bound, across frozen Lake Bennett.

the wood piled on the sled, the canvas water bag hanging from a tent pole, the suitable dress of the stampeders, and the cooking utensils.

Boatbuilding at this cove at Lake Bennett was retarded by the lack of timber.

Here boats are nearing completion at Abbott's Cove, Lake Bennett. The snow is gone. Soon the ice on the lake will crumble and crack and the waters will run free. When that happens—usually in late May or early June—the boats must be ready to carry the men and their supplies on to the gold fields.

Approximately eight hundred feet of lumber was required for a boat suitable to carry a ton of freight. When Mike King arrived and assembled a knockdown sawmill, stampeders welcomed the chance to work, for lumber brought up to $350 per thousand feet. Mounted police passed freely among the boat builders, advising them on their building and how to navigate the Yukon, "Build strong. Don't start out in a floating coffin."

Hundreds of boats preparing to set out across Lake Bennett for the gold fields.

"Headed for the gold fields." The Hegg boat flies a flag.

5

Down

The Yukon

STAMPEDERS OVER the Chilkoot Trail and those over White Pass met and merged at Lake Bennett, a twenty-five-mile waterway that dwindled into a stream which in turn poured into Tagish Lake. Another stream led to shallow Lake Marsh. Below Lake Marsh were the swift waters of Miles Canyon and White Horse Rapids. Then came Lake LaBerge, Thirty Mile River, and Five Finger Rapids where stampeders would be still nearly two hundred and fifty miles from Dawson. The only really rough water ahead was at Rink Rapids. Otherwise there were just the wide, open waters of the main stem of the Yukon River.

On May 30, 1898, the ice broke on Lake Bennett, and the next day eight hundred boats set out for the Klondike. It was here at Lake Bennett that the author's father, Peter B. ("P.B.") Anderson, built a boat for Eric Hegg, with a cabin for a "dark room" that would be especially suited to photographic purposes.

On June 1, the Hegg party, consisting of Eric, his brother Pete, P.B., and a Mr. Grant who had joined them, started down the lake in two boats. Prior to the gold rush, Grant had sailed on whaling vessels off the coast of Siberia.

It was calm when the Hegg party left, but eight miles out, a storm arose. They hoisted sails and fairly flew across the water. The wind increased. A tarpaulin—stretched across the top of Eric's boat, at Mr. Grant's insistence—kept the boat from swamping as the waves washed over it. Other boats driven down the lake were not so fortunate. Many piled up on the beaches, and floating luggage told of tragedy; but the Hegg boats maneuvered to shore, where the men dried their supplies.

These boats are sailing down Lake Marsh, Klondike bound. By clever manipulation of sail and oars, stampeders could gain on the boat ahead—gain on their fellows and their chances for finding claims. Note the sail specks in the distance and smoke from a forest fire which raged in the pitchy spruce forests.

On they came, through river and lake, the thousands of gold seekers, pouring their energy into a wild stampede for gold.

In the summer of 1898, the black line of stampeders stretched back across the rivers, lakes, mountains, and oceans to an excited world awaiting the news that their loved ones had "struck it rich."

Many a stampeder leaving Bennett before the lakes and rivers cleared found himself caught among the cakes of ice, jammed by the swift current of flood time. Drifting helplessly among the swirling floes, boats were crushed like match boxes. The immense scows below, loaded with supplies and mining machinery, were caught in the ice at Lake Marsh in June 1899.

Thwarted thus, gold seekers found time to appraise the country to which they had come. A land of great opportunity and a wealth of resources unfolded before them. Industries which flourished to the south could flourish here. Where the moose fattened, beef cattle would also fatten. Where the Indians trapped furs, the white man could do likewise. It was a raw new land to be had for the taking.

Over-eager stampeders were caught in great swirls of ice floes on Lake Marsh, whose waters were so shallow that they were the last to thaw out in the spring break-up.

Herds of caribou provided welcome fresh meat for the gold seekers.

Having reached the interior of Canada, the argonauts were able to supplement their food supply from the land itself. Moose roamed the lowlands. Bear hunted the streams. Mountain goat and ptarmigan wandered among the mountain crags. Great flocks of geese and mallards nested along the lakes. Greyling and trout were plentiful for the taking. And herds of caribou, trailing like a brown ribbon five miles long and a mile wide, fed their way south and north again; hence the name Caribou Crossing. Without the tundra moss as food, the caribou could not exist. Giving a sideward motion of the head they push aside the snow and dig with a spatula-like horn that protrudes from their forehead.

It was here at Caribou Crossing (Carcross) that George Carmack, who filed Discovery Claim on Bonanza Creek, married Kate, the beautiful Indian girl. Shortly after the gold rush she returned to her own people at Carcross, among the mountains and rivers she loved. Though she lived in a simple log cabin and dressed in cheap cotton dresses, she always wore a necklace made from nuggets she had picked up on Discovery Claim. On the walls of her humble home were pictures of the King and Queen of England. The Canadian government rewarded her with a pension for her part in the discovery of Klondike gold. Kate Carmack loved to visit with old friends and talk over the days when she was a millionaire's wife and traveled far to the south. She had soon tired of the bustling cities, though, and never forgot how she had resorted to Indian trail-blazing by carving notches on the hotel banister so she could find her way back to her room. Kate Carmack died in 1917 or 1918.

Caribou Crossing.

The approach to treacherous Miles Canyon.

When the stampeders reached Miles Canyon —twenty-three miles below Lake Marsh—they tied up to the bank just above the canyon to survey the swift water ahead.

It was here at the upper end of the canyon that two partners fell into disagreement. Not being able to settle their dispute amicably, they divided the outfit, sawed the boat in two, and separated.

Miles Canyon, one of the most dangerous stretches in the North, has walls forty to a hundred feet high, and the river that pours through is a hundred feet wide. Because of its swift current and great volume of water, the rise in the middle hogbacks from two to four feet higher than on the sides.

Boats were held to the crest of the current where the speed of the current spewed them on

their way. Once a boat slipped from this crest, the backwash and whirlpools crushed it against the rocks. In the early days of the Klondike gold rush, "greenhorns" lost up to two hundred boats a week. Later, Mounted Police forbade boats to pass through Miles Canyon and White Horse Rapids without an experienced pilot.

Two miles below Miles Canyon, White Horse Rapids presented another dangerous piece of water. Pilots received $25 and up to take a boat or scow through the White Horse. Freight was soaked as boats nose-dived over submerged rocks and careened in the whirlpools. The many crosses on the banks of the Yukon were grim reminders of tragedy. The lower shore was lined with boats which had stopped to salvage and dry out food. Many stampeders lowered their boats through the rapids with ropes and portaged their supplies.

Town of White Horse in 1900.

Miles Canyon (above) and White Horse Rapids (below) are two of the most dangerous stretches of water in the North.

This tramline (right) was later built to bypass Miles Canyon and White Horse Rapids. The Gleaner, Australian, and Nora are shown docked at the pole wharf to load freight and passengers.

When Norman Macauley and his party came to Miles Canyon and White Horse Rapids, they immediately conceived the idea of building a tramline to circumvent the three miles of dangerous water. Tracks were made of hewed poles. The flat beds, horse drawn, efficiently hauled tons of supplies and saved the lives of hundreds who might have dared the rapids and the canyon in order to reach the Klondike ahead of the thousands they knew were on the way.

For five cents a pound, the Miles Canyon and White Horse Rapids Tramway carried goods from above the canyon to White Horse. Endless lives were thus saved, but many men who had mortgaged their very lives to buy grubstakes and join this frenzied race found any fee impossible to pay.

Here the steamer, *Casca,* on the Upper Yukon, is carrying a hundred and fifty tons of freight.

These lake and river boats were of a flat-bottomed construction. The cargo booms, also called jetson poles, were used to free the boat from the shifting sandbars. By means of pulleys and cables, the booms were lowered onto the bars, and as the boat was propelled ahead, the bow of the boat was lifted from the bar. At the peak of the lift the engines were reversed and the boat slid off. Iron shoes were attached to the booms by means of a collar which prevented them from sinking into the sand.

Most of these steamers had a draft of about thirty-eight inches. Each ton lowered the boat into the water about an inch. The barges which they pushed often measured a hundred feet, carried about a hundred and thirty tons, and had a draft of about forty inches. Captains "jack-knifed" the barges ahead of them by means of ropes and tackles. Great skill was displayed in pushing one, two, and sometimes three barges ahead of the steamer.

Just before the fall freeze-up, steamers were taken out of the river to protect them from damage by river ice. Overhauled and repainted, they brought fresh supplies and mail to eager inhabitants along the Yukon, when the ice went out.

← *The Miles Canyon and White Horse Rapids Tramway. Note the freight piled to the right in the picture, awaiting transportation. The log cabins of the Mounted Police can be seen in the center background.*

The steamer, *A. J. Goddard,* returned from Dawson to White Horse on the Upper Yukon, on July 4, 1898, with the first passengers, their gold, and the Crown mail. Captain Goddard had landed in Dyea in 1897 with a sawmill and the steamers, *J. H. Kilbourne* and *A. J. Goddard,* built in San Francisco by the Upper Yukon Company. The bulky machinery and hulls, knocked down, were freighted over Chilkoot Pass by the pack train and aerial tramline and assembled on the ways at Lake Bennett. When Mrs. Goddard came up for a visit later, she found hundreds of stampeders bedridden with typhoid fever, Captain Goddard among them. She immediately stepped into the emergency, nursing, washing, cooking, and baking bread on a typical small Klondike stove. She kept the men's time and paid them off. The pioneer way of life crowded her days, but a love of the North was born; and her visit of a few weeks lengthened into years.

The Alaska Commercial Company, with general offices in San Francisco, bought out the Russian-American Company in 1867 and established stations at all the principal points in Alaska. By 1869 a passenger-and-freight boat made a regular run on the Yukon River. Having a thirty-year background of occupation, the Alaska Commercial Company was able to outfit the men with the kind of clothing and provisions

The A. J. Goddard *out of Dawson.*

best suited to the country. Invariably supplies included some protection against the mosquitoes of the Yukon, one of the greatest irritations suffered by the stampeders.

Terror tales of the Chilkoot Trail and Skagway, pictures of dead horses, frozen mountain peaks, and the dread of a swollen Yukon forced many gold seekers to wait for passage on the steamers sailing from Nome to Dawson— the *Alice,* the *Louise,* the *Yukon,* the new steel sidewheeler the *Sadie,* the *Hannah,* the *Sarah,* and the *Monarch.* There was no delay along the river; wood was already cut and piled at convenient points en route. The steamers were fast and commodious; the captains reliable, having had years of experience.

A steamer "lines up" through Five Finger Rapids in the picture below. It was not a dangerous passage but a narrow one, and larger craft could assume the right-of-way. Here the steamer being roped upriver clearly had the advantage over the smaller craft.

The end of a cable anchored upstream was fastened to the capstan on the prow of the boat.

As the cable wound around the capstan, the boat moved slowly against the current up the river. Once out of swift water, the boat could proceed on its own power.

The scow to the left is loaded with gold seekers, headed downriver for Dawson. Note the long sweeps by which the scow is cleverly maneuvered into the current.

Running the rapids.

The E. A. Hegg party prepares supper on the banks of the Yukon. Note the mosquito netting on their hats and the cabin dark room where Mr. Hegg developed pictures.

Many of these scows had facilities for cooking aboard, but the smaller boats meant camping on shore to cook. Meals were prepared on the popular collapsible Klondike stove. During the period of the midnight sun, they could travel safely twenty-four hours a day.

The Hegg boat arrives at the mouth of Stewart River. Note the photographer's furled canvas sign. In 1885, the sand bars of the Stewart had yielded 2,500 pounds of gold dust. In 1897 and 1898, many of the stampeders turned up the Stewart River on prospecting tours.

At Stewart City, the Hegg party learned that timber was scarce in Dawson. So, while the noted photographer was reconnoitering for views of the land, partners Anderson and Grant went ashore and cut timber for house logs. When these were rafted and towed downstream to Dawson, businessmen gladly paid $80 a log. Later on, stampeders who were disappointed in staking a claim for themselves found the wood business quite profitable.

This canoe, in danger of being crushed between ice floes running in the Yukon River, has been pulled on an ice floe for safety. Once out in the swift current it was impossible to direct a landing and many boats were swept miles past the Klondike.

Stampeders hoping to get transportation on river steamers found fares raised beyond their means. An item in the *Klondike News* of April 1, 1898, gave the following warning: "If you think of going to Dawson by any of these lines, take two years' supplies and a gatling gun, for they never will land you as long as they have bar fixtures, whiskey, and billiard tables to transport."

This was the post of the Northwest Mounted Police at the mouth of Stewart River. The roof of the log cabin is covered with slabs, dirt, and canvas. Paddle and pike poles for use along the river lean against the wall. Every passing boat was required to check in at every post stationed along the river. Should a pilot forget, a shot fired across the bow of his boat would be a reminder.

"... the bank of the Yukon was a ragged scallop of boats and scows...."

Around a grand curve of the Yukon lay Dawson City. As far as gold seekers could see, the bank of the Yukon was a ragged scallop of boats and scows, jammed tight together, end to end, three and four deep. Lumber from dismantled dories and scows was in great demand for fuel and building purposes. The Klondike River separated Dawson from the Indian village, "Louse Town." The muskeg swamp swarmed with bewildered argonauts asking, "Where do we go to dig gold?" The place was alive with dogs mooching at grub stakes. Here and there pack trains loafed in the mire or moved slowly out of town overloaded with mining needs and food.

When Hegg arrived in Dawson to set up another studio, in the summer of 1898, there were some forty thousand persons in or about the town; and the first wild excitement of gold discovery had subsided. For the most part, the individual gold panner was being superseded by the mining company.

It was a conglomerate community of trampled mud streets, saloons, gambling houses, log houses, and dance halls.

Could this be the Dawson whose story had circled the globe and sent men rushing northward in quest of sudden wealth?

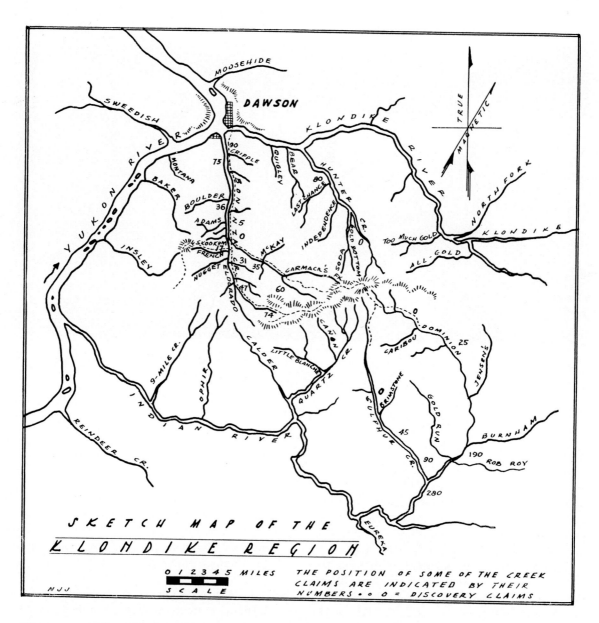

This map of the Klondike shows the various hills and creeks which produced $100,000,000 between 1898 and 1905, within a fifteen-mile radius. By the spring of 1899, all the creeks of any importance in the Klondike area had been staked.

6

Dawson

and the

Gold Fields

THE KLONDIKE gold rush was a great level-er. A man's past was forgotten and no questions were asked. His speech might betray him but never his clothes, for the millionaire and the hired man dressed alike. On Hunker Creek, three lawyers, three doctors, a sea captain, and a preacher mucked together in a smoky shaft.

Dawson cared nothing about who you were or where you came from. Dawson asked, "What can you do?" There was wood to cut; there were logs to haul, and cabins to build. There was food to cook and there were dishes to wash—and spittoons to clean. Miners fresh from a clean-up tossed nuggets into the cuspidors and laughed as "down-and-outers" fished them from the "snoose" and tobacco juice.

That was the Dawson of 1898—a place of intense joy and a place of bitter disappointment. Most men had forgotten that two years had passed since George Carmack's great discovery on Bonanza Creek.

Back to Dawson stumbled the failures, back to signs which read, "Help Wanted. Miners, $15 per day. Wood cutters—cooks—carpenters. *Bring your own grub.*" Back they came to a few weeks' work for the fare home; back to sell their outfits; back to Dawson with its circus atmosphere, carnival noises, sawdust-covered floors, and saloons.

Everywhere Dawson had some reminder of the new Eldorado: gold scales; streams of yellow dust; picks and shovels; moosehide pokes, some large, some small enough for a man's pocket. Miners with radiant faces and hearty laughter—their gumboots caked with slimy muck—tossed nuggets and pokes of gold dust across the bars. But, by 1899, for the great majority the mirage was fading, both rainbow and the pot of gold.

The Dawson waterfront in 1899.

Those who stampeded over Chilkoot and down the Yukon in 1899 found that they had arrived too late; all the best ground had been staked. They had to buy claims, fractions of claims, or work for wages. The following winter was a long, hungry one for 10,000 destitute men in Dawson.

Dawson's Front Street in 1899 was a row of flimsy tents and cabins. In the picture above, scows have just arrived along the river front with much-needed produce and freight. Rafts of logs have been brought from upriver for fuel and cabins. No loiterers appear along the bank; gold seekers were busy finding some niche for themselves in the bustling new city.

Every cabin had a small plank trough filled with water in which a miner regularly tested the dirt from his shaft. In this way he knew how close he was to bedrock and in which direction he should work. He also obtained gold for his immediate needs as the winter passed.

Below is a typical miner's cabin with its home-made bunks, armchair, and stool. A pair of work pants, well patched, shows at the left. Note the orderliness of everything—the books on the shelf, the neatly piled wood, and the frying pans on the wall. The miner in the foreground hides the Klondike stove, but on the shelf above it can be seen the coffee pot and a can of sourdough.

Miners making a test of gold-bearing gravel.

70

Gold nugget that weighed nearly five pounds.

Gold nuggets weighing up to seventy-seven ounces were found on Cheechako Hill by Saples and Small, and gold was mined in fabulous quantities along the Klondike creeks. No fewer than twenty-nine pack horses waddled into Dawson in one day in June 1899, from the clean-up of Alexander McDonald, who was supposed to have been worth $7,000,000 at one time.

In 1896, Klondike creeks produced $300,000; in 1897, $2,500,000; in 1898, $10,000,000; in 1899, $16,000,000; and in 1900, $22,275,000.

In Dawson and along the creeks, gold was used as legal tender. Every man carried his poke of dust, which was weighed in scales in payment for his purchase. All nickels, dimes, and pennies were tossed into a box behind the counter—for nothing sold that cheaply.

After Carmack's strike on the Bonanza, Joseph Ladue—who had operated a sawmill in conjunc-

tion with his trading post at Forty-Mile—moved both store and mill to Dawson. Besides lumber for commercial buildings and cabins, one of the most sought-after products of Ladue's mill was sluice boxes. For a time, Carmack himself was employed at Ladue's mill to help pay for the material needed to work his Discovery claim.

To William Ogilvie goes credit for exploring and first surveying the Canadian-American boundary. After the United States purchased Alaska in 1867, many people in the Klondike area didn't know if they were on Canadian or American soil.

The Klondike gold rush started shortly after Ogilvie had completed the boundary survey. Later he returned to straighten out the tangle of claims; he had a rare talent for creating order. Working out of his headquarters at Forty-Mile—just twenty-five miles from the boundary line—Ogilvie measured out exact footages of claims.

"Tagish" Charlie (above) and "Skookum" Jim (below), Indian in-laws of George Carmack, were with him at the time of discovery.

"Tagish" Charlie, sometimes called "Cultus," was a brother-in-law of George Carmack. He staked Claim No. 2 below Discovery on the Bonanza, and registered his claim, along with Carmack, in September 1896. As a reward for his part in the discovery of Klondike gold, he was given Canadian citizenship and the white man's privilege of entering a saloon. He was proud of this distinction and enjoyed calling for "treats for the house" with the result that he spent much time in the "Skookum House" or jail. "Skookum" means strong. While returning home from a holiday celebration, Charlie fell from the bridge of the White Pass Railroad at Carcross and was drowned.

"Skookum" Jim, who also registered a claim on the Bonanza in that eventful fall of 1896, was an excellent prospector. On his trips, which sometimes lasted several weeks, he carried only a gold pan, a pick, a rifle, and a hatchet — the rifle for food and the hatchet for shelter. The nickname Skookum, or strong, was given him because he once carried a hundred and sixty pounds of bacon over Chilkoot on a single trip.

"Skookum" Jim poses with his pick.

The claims of George Carmack, "Skookum" Jim, and "Tagish" Charlie are in the foreground. Each claim measured five hundred feet along the creek and extended across the valley from rimrock to rimrock. Since the gold here lay close to the surface, they shoveled the gravel directly into the sluice boxes. Note the slender timbers supporting the sluice box as it extends over the rectangular surface mine. As the excavation deepened, the gravel was shoveled from one platform to another until the sluice box could be reached. Later on, shafts were sunk. Still later, the entire valley was dredged.

In staking a placer claim such as Carmack's, the law demanded that two posts, numbered one and two respectively, be planted firmly in the ground on base lines at each end of the claim, with a line well cleared between the two posts. The posts had to be at least four feet high, and flattened on two sides for a distance of at least a foot from the top, with a face of four inches and a diameter of not less than five inches. On the side of each post facing the claim, the name and number of the claim had to be legibly written, the date when staked, and the full Christian and surname of the locator. A tree or stump cut off, flattened and faced to proper height and size, could be used as a post. Much disorder and trouble arose along the Klondike creeks because stampeders did not acquaint themselves with mining laws.

Facsimile of George Washington Carmack's application for his Discovery Claim on Bonanza Creek. He was to "acquire the land for the sole purpose of mining." Captain Constantine signed the application, September 24, 1896.

Claim No. 2, below Discovery on the Bonanza —operated by "Tagish" Charlie—rated next to the Discovery claim of Carmack. Bonanza, however, was generally richer above Carmack's claim than below.

Small tramcars hauled the gold-laden gravel up an incline and dumped it into the sluice box. The water rushing along dissolved the clump of dirt and washed the rocks, freeing the gold which, being heavier, dropped and was caught in the aprons lining the bottom of the sluice box. The tailings—clean rock—were shoveled out.

Sunset on Gold Hill.

Gold pan and first gold taken out of his Gold Hill claim by Nathan Kresge, co-discoverer with Nels Peterson.

In the great rush there was no time to prospect. It was assumed that all creeks were as rich as Bonanza and that it was only necessary to acquire a claim to become a millionaire. Gold seekers paid thousands of dollars for claims which proved to be blanks. Not realizing that mining is expensive, many men became discouraged, sold out for what they could get, and took the first boat available for the outside, never knowing that their claim had been a producer.

When "greenhorns" arrived and cried, "Show me the way!" old-timers winked slyly and said, "Try the hills!"

Overnight a row of bench claims circled the hills as prospectors burrowed like gophers into the frozen ground. From the valleys came an echo, "Look! Cheechako Hill!"

In the fall of 1897, a Seattle sawmill worker, Oliver Millett, made one of the greatest strikes of the gold rush on Cheechako Hill, by figuring out the course of the ancient stream that had enriched both Eldorado and Bonanza. He demonstrated that a clever cheechako could outwit a veteran sourdough in the game for gold.

How could miners with their fabulously rich valley claims know that, in eons past, nature had up-ended the country, completely changing the course of the White River, and that the hilltops as well as the valley cradled her old bed with its hidden gold? And Cheechako Hill proved the richest hill of all.

This gold pan contains the first gold Nathan Kresge took out of his Gold Hill claim. On the day of discovery, Kresge and his partner, Nels Peterson, picked up $29 in coarse gold, almost on the surface of the ground. In the course of ten days they rocked out $6,375 from a claim one hundred feet square. Their success stimulated the rush to other hills which had been considered blanks. Caribou Bill, an old miner from British Columbia, hearing of Kresge's luck, grubstaked a number of men to test the hill slopes. They found gold on Little Skookum and French Hill. The stampede for the hills—any hill—became general and by the summer of 1898 work had been begun on all the high levels. Every foot of every hill—Gold Hill, French Hill, and Adams—was staked and worked by some frenzied stampeder. By 1899, mining operations in the Klondike were yielding millions of dollars.

This picture, taken from Claim No. 8 on Bonanza, and looking down the Bonanza stream, shows the valley village of Grand Forks, which sprang up at the mouth of the Eldorado. Beyond is Gold Hill with its tier of bench claims.

Mouth of the Klondike River at midnight. A footbridge crossed the Klondike River and connected Dawson with Louse Town, later called Klondike City.

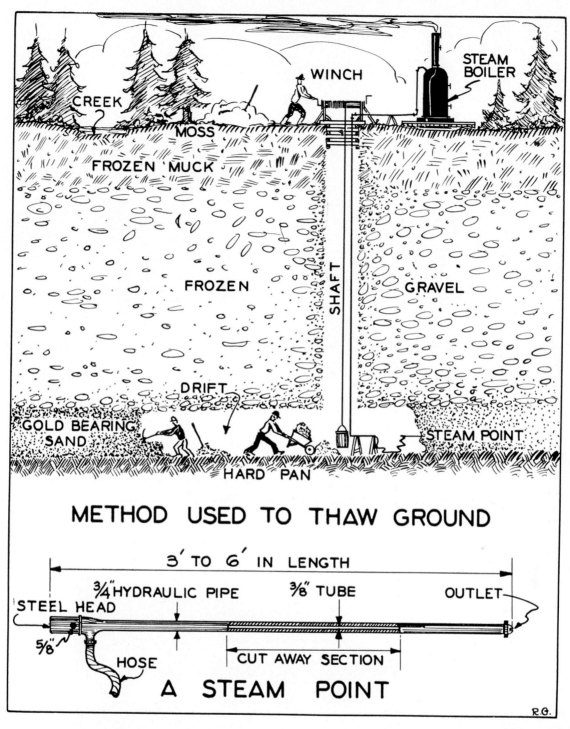

METHOD USED TO THAW GROUND

3′ TO 6′ IN LENGTH

STEEL HEAD — ¾″ HYDRAULIC PIPE — ⅜″ TUBE — OUTLET

5/8″ — HOSE — CUT AWAY SECTION

A STEAM POINT

R.G.

In the Klondike district the ground is frozen to bedrock at depths ranging from fifteen to forty feet below the surface. This forced miners to devise new methods of mining, as previous experiences in other camps were of little benefit. The first miners used wood fires to sink their shafts to bedrock. A fire about six feet long and four feet wide was built on the ground and allowed to burn eight or ten hours. Then the ground which was thawed was dug out. Another fire was started in the hole, followed in ten hours by another excavation.

By alternate thawing and digging, the shaft was sunk to bedrock at the rate of two or three feet for each fire. In most cases, some kind of frame or retaining wall was necessary. When bedrock, or hardpan, was reached, the miner opened his passageway to the gold-bearing vein by continued means of fire, hoisting out the gravel and bedrock formation containing the gold. This work was usually done in winter. When the ice became liquid in the spring, sluicing was begun. Eventually miners replaced fires for thawing with steam points; the steam was generated by a boiler at the surface.

These miners are rocking for gold on Gold Hill. Water, which was scarce, was used again and again. Pay dirt was shoveled into the perforated tray and water was poured over it while the rocker was cradled from side to side. The gold washed through the holes in the tray to be caught in aprons within the box-like device, and the water poured out into the wooden tank to be used another time. Note the windlass and the shaft at the left-hand side; also the dump of pay dirt picked and hoisted to the surface the previous winter. In the valley below Gold Hill is the village of Grand Forks, where the children went to school in 1899 and where the miners had their frolic when the day's work was over.

The Magnet Road House on Bonanza

Miss Belinda Mulrooney built the first road-house on the creeks at Grand Forks, with the aid of a broken-down mule, and she called it The Magnet. Dawsonites laughed at her for building so far away from Dawson, but she proved that when men were hungry and thirsty they would stop at the first available place. Through the long winter nights, the Magnet's big pot-bellied stove grew redder and redder, fed by huge chunks of pitchy spruce. In one corner a man with a mouth organ played "After the Ball Was Over," and dance-hall girls cheered the new-made millionaires as they danced the muck of their claims from their boots. Outside, the blizzard whined and the lone wolf howled.

Children also became gold minded. Each had his own little "rocker" where he spent many hours scraping up pay dirt which the miners left in indentations in the ground. They carried dirt, dipped water, cradled the rocker, and were delighted at the first gleams of yellow gold. Fourteen dollars' worth of gold was discovered on their peak day. Great excitement prevailed when one pupil found a nugget as large as a dollar, and almost as thin, plastered to a piece of shale by the muck formation.

Pupils and teacher pose in front of the Grand Forks schoolhouse, the first school in the Klondike. The author is the towhead in the dark dress.

Young prospector pauses and poses for the camera on Magnet Hill.

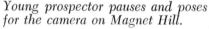

Note how the creek bed here at French Hill is crisscrossed with sluice boxes and piles of tailings scattered beside them. When Photographer Hegg took this picture, the sluicing season was over for the year. Next winter other shafts would be dug.

The royalty on all gold shipped from the Yukon was 2½ per cent, or 37½ cents per ounce. The valuation of gold for royalty purposes was $15 an ounce.

In pack trains such as this one on Cheechako Hill, each horse carried approximately $20,000; and it was not uncommon for a pack train to bring out $100,000 for a clean-up. These shipments were always guarded by police and owners. The gold was stored with firms in Dawson until shipped on the first available boat.

The Porcupine Mining Company is here at work below Discovery. Pay dirt was close to the surface and was shoveled from platform to platform and finally into the sluice box, where the gold was separated from the dirt. Gold varied greatly as to grade, not only on the different creeks but along different portions of the same creek. One versed in the ways of gold could frequently tell where it was mined by its appearance. Native gold is alloyed with silver in varying proportions.

A tier of mines half way up Cheechako Hill, a rich district. The piles of dirt awaited to be sluiced when the spring thaw came. The long poles were used for the frozen shafts. Mining operations were not intensive in 1897. In 1898, they began to show their real colors. In 1899, they were yielding millions in real gold. Mines on Cheechako Hill, Gold Hill, and Adams, just above Bonanza Creek, were great producers.

Looking up Eldorado, the richest valley in the Klondike.

Eldorado Creek was literally a channel of gold. Not a blank claim was found on its four-mile length and most of the claims were fabulously rich. In 1898, $10,000,000 was sluiced out from the Klondike creeks.

This picture looks up Eldorado, the richest valley in the Klondike, with its cabins, shafts, sluice boxes, piles of tailings, muck, and water. Shown in the foreground are flat-topped dumps not yet sluiced. The best pan of gravel washed out netted $700 and came from the crevices of bedrock. Eldorado gold was largely of nugget form. The first two years of mining produced $200,000 per year. A half interest in Claim No. 9 once sold for $800. The lower half of this claim, when worked intensively through the winter of 1897 and 1898, produced a net output of a quarter of a million dollars. In 1899, No. 9 was valued at one million dollars. (The author's father hauled wood for miners in Eldorado Valley.)

In early spring, onions, radishes and lettuce and flowers were planted in the dirt which covered the roofs of the cabins. The heat from the inside forced growth.

The miner in the foreground proudly displays two large nuggets of gold in his pan. Sometimes, when bedrock was reached, nuggets and gold dust lay like a yellow sheet, more gold than gravel.

Charlie Anderson, a Swede, earned and saved $600 as a pick-and-shovel man at the bottom of such a shaft as this. The work was hard and a celebration was in order. Buying a bottle of whiskey, he invited two old prospectors to help him celebrate. That night Anderson paid his $600 of hard-earned gold dust for their claim. The next morning he awakened with a headache and their worthless claim on upper Eldorado.

"Vell," Anderson observed, "I better go to vork." He went down into the shaft. The dump of pay dirt grew. Not long afterward, while he was testing a pan of dirt, the two men passed him on their way to Dawson. With a sly wink at each other, they asked if he had found anything.

"Ay tank ay got some gold here," Anderson replied. In the gold pan was $1,400. Had the men dug two feet deeper to bedrock, the $1,250,000 which the claim yielded would have been theirs.

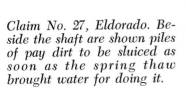

Claim No. 27, Eldorado. Beside the shaft are shown piles of pay dirt to be sluiced as soon as the spring thaw brought water for doing it.

Underground on Claim No. 27, Eldorado.

Fourth tier of Gold Hill, opposite Claim No. 5, Bonanza.

At day's end came the inevitable pork and beans.

All winter long, the miner thawed the dirt, shoveled it out and thawed it again. The gold-laden gravel was hoisted to the top where it lay until summer, when water was available for sluicing.

Mining in the Klondike was peculiar to that district. Ages ago, gold deposits to a depth of twelve to fifty feet were locked in frozen gravel and debris. Some miners preferred to pick the surface dirt loose in its frozen state. Others preferred using fires to thaw the muck. Below the muck, thawing and restraining walls were necessary. The scarcity of candles and wood hampered the early miners in sinking their shafts.

In 1898, candles cost a dollar each; cabins held more gold than food, and miners gladly paid a dollar for one whirl around the dance hall with a dance-hall queen in his arms. Every spring, a French woman arrived in Dawson with an elaborate assortment of gowns by Worth of Paris. And what millionaire would begrudge a thousand-dollar dress for his lady-love? Or diamonds? Or rubies?

And sometimes into the dance halls drifted men who were lonesome, so heartsick that they were willing to pay almost any price just to sit and talk to a girl who understood how they felt, who knew, or seemed to know, what it was to yearn for the sight of the old farm or to sit again in Mom's spicy kitchen.

At the end of the day miners sat down at a crude table to a fare of beans and salt pork—or salt pork and beans. In the craze for gold they dared to remain in that deep smoky shaft for long hours. Bodies grew gaunt and aching as the importance of gold overruled the need for food.

It was for this that they had climbed old Chilkoot or struggled through the White Pass . . . Not today . . . not tomorrow . . . but perhaps next June, when the sun melted glaciers for sluicing, would theirs be the great clean-up.

Dawson was clearly a "man's town." The huge banner stretching across the shop fronts announces that the Steamers Eldorado *and* Bonanza King *will get them to Seattle and Vancouver, B. C., in 10 days.*

The dog, so essential to the life of the North, was to Klondikers what the covered wagon and pack horse were to the Forty-niners of California. A sled weighed sixty pounds. The load for each dog was approximately a hundred and fifty pounds. An animal in good trim could travel eight hours a day. Always in the forefront when needed for work, the dog did his share in settling the country. He endured the same hardships as the prospector, worked with him and starved with him. In many cases he furnished food for him; in a few cases he died with him, and in one case he made a gold discovery while digging a rabbit out of a root hole.

The Northern Commercial Company at Dawson gave a stabilizing influence to the North, trading, buying, and selling. Here the employees and company freight teams are lined up in impressive array for the photographer.

Miners awaiting their turn to register claims at Dawson. Claims had to be staked and registered and a sample of gold shown. This line of men might have been waiting hours to register.

"One of the chief duties of the Northwest Mounted Police was to stop the sale of liquor to the Indians and to provide medical care, medicine, and food for the sick and destitute."

The champion hose team of Dawson.

Burning of Dawson, 1898

Dawson had several serious fires in its early history. The log cabins with moss chinking and the cold weather which called for red-hot stoves made the city a potential tinderbox. With the installation of a water system and the organization of a fire department, every building within the fire limit was visited at least once a month. A written report was made, detailing the conditions, the means of heating, lighting, and the type of occupancy. Every stove, furnace, and smoke pipe received rigid examination. Twenty-four hours was the time limit in making requested changes.

As a result of this attention to preventing fires, there was little loss until the day Dawson burned. This fatal fire, which ate the core out of the town, was caused when a dance-hall girl in a fit of temper threw a lighted lamp at a rival. To prevent the recurrence of such a holocaust, all undesirable women were moved to Louse Town, later called Klondike City, across the Klondike River from Dawson . . .

. . . and this picture by omnipresent Photographer Hegg shows the midnight hour in Oshiwora, or "White Chapel," in Louse Town, where these women were sent.

A ton and a half of gold bricks and gold dust, piled in the Alaska Commercial Store, awaits arrival of the boat.

Dust was melted in the bank's assay office. The base metals—iron and copper—were fluxed off in the process. The gold was then poured into bar molds and allowed to cool. Thoroughly cleansed of slag, the bars were weighed; and the original weight of ore dust and the new weight of the bar represented the loss in melting. The average loss in the case of clean, bright dust was about two per cent.

The bars were then chipped—the chippings being taken from top and bottom—and assayed. The results were given in points of "fineness,"

with "1,000 fine" representing pure gold at $20.67 per ounce. Gold was the only metal which was not subject to the variations of price with market fluctuations.

By 1900, the first rare atmosphere of the gold rush was gone. Dawson had taken on the qualities of a city. Stampeders with diversified abilities and inclinations had been absorbed into the city or had returned disillusioned to the outside world and home. Mining corporations had arrived with dredges and modern machinery, their representatives buying up every claim which could be bought. Large flumes insured the water so necessary for mining; no poor man could afford to bring water from such distances.

Gold waiting for shipment on the dock at Dawson. These boxes, heavily reinforced with steel bands, required the services of two men to be lifted. The gold in these boxes contained an estimated $1,500,000.

Dawson in 1900—a thriving metropolis at the junction of the Klondike and Yukon rivers. In four years, Dawson had grown from a muskeg swamp to a well-organized city because some fifty thousand stampeders had landed on the banks of the Yukon to search for Klondike gold.

One of the '98ers immortalized by E. A. Hegg.

Concerning Eric A. Hegg, Photographer

Few men leave a memorial of such increasing value as did Eric A. Hegg, the photographer who joined the great stampede to the Klondike in 1897.

Hegg was born at Bollnas, Sweden, on September 17, 1867, according to his son, Roy E. Hegg. While Eric was still a small lad, the family migrated to the United States and settled in Wisconsin. After several years studying art and photography, he opened his first studio in Washburn, Wisconsin, at the age of fifteen.

With the extension of transcontinental railways, the entire East was rolling up a healthy curiosity about the Pacific Coast. Drawn by stories of trees eight and ten feet in diameter, mountains tumbling snowcapped peaks the length of a coastline, great rivers of salmon trailing silver ribbons through the ocean, and opportunity knocking loud at every man's door, young Hegg, in 1888, tucked his camera under his arm and joined the great western migration.

He arrived in Tacoma, Washington. After a short stay, he boarded the steamer *Fairhaven* on her maiden voyage to New Whatcom (now Bellingham). There he stayed, setting up a studio on the corner of State and Holly streets, where the Alaska Building presently stands. A year later he opened another studio in Fairhaven, one of the four rival communities situated around the protected harbor of the bay.

Business was good in those boom days of 1889. Logging camps had begun to chew at the great forests. Along the skid roads, which serpentined through the dense woods, strings of oxen pulled the big logs to the water. Mills belched forth piles of lumber and bundles of shingles. The whine of saws, the whir of machinery, and the mill whistles, morning, noon and night, spread a feeling of cheer that all was well in this new land. Fishing brought sockeye, humpback, and king salmon to the cannery at Fairhaven, one of the largest in the world. Windjammers and schooners, with an aura of foreign shores, loaded the products of forest and sea and sailed away to return for more cargo.

E. A. Hegg was a wiry chap and an excellent hiker. No part of the country but what knew his step; no industry but what had stopped its wheels while he focused his camera.

Newcomers, desirous of urging the remnants of eastern families to come to "God's Country," sent them Hegg pictures of every phase of life and living.

In 1893, the panic sent black clouds of depression across the country. Business slackened like the sails of a ship when the wind is gone. Mill whistles no longer greeted the dawn. Canneries closed. Dollars disappeared. Men brought out their guns, their fishrods and berry buckets, and lived again from the land itself. Through these dark days, Hegg carried on, for babies grow old and bridal days must be remembered; a favorite ox team may die and the largest tree be sawed up.

Then, gold was discovered in the Klondike, and a country less known than even the Pacific Northwest called. Hegg could not resist the urge to follow. Leasing the *Skagit Chief*, a river boat of long renown, E. A. Hegg and a group of stampeders headed for Dyea, the gateway to the Klondike. Loaded to the gunwales and under tow, the *Skagit Chief* began a hazardous trip up the Alaskan Coast. In Hegg's words, "How we ever made that trip seems an act of Providence.

We encountered terrible storms. Battered by the wind and wave, the boat quivered until we thought it would break up at any moment. Once the tow line broke and we lurched toward the rocks. We fought for our lives."

The *Skagit Chief* reached Dyea in the fall of 1897—too late for Hegg to make the trip down-river to Dawson before the winter freeze-up. While he was still in Dyea, Hegg was joined by his younger brother, Pete; and P. B. Anderson, the author's father. The three pooled their money; and it was agreed that Anderson and young Hegg would cross the mountains and build a boat at Lake Bennett for the trip down-river in the spring—while Eric stayed on in Dyea and earned money taking pictures.

Hegg immediately set up an impromptu studio in Dyea. This first photographic studio in the North was built from the remains of scows that had washed ashore. Because the makeshift build-ing let in light as well as rain, Hegg erected a tent in one corner for developing his photograph-ic plates.

"Taking pictures was then the hardest kind of work," Hegg relates. "I had to pack food, cloth-ing, and shelter as well as pack and protect my equipment. Equipment was very cumbersome and bulky then. It was no sinecure to develop and print pictures in a tent, with a blizzard howling and freezing. Many times the cold in the tent became so intense that the developer would have to be heated; and before the pic-tures were printed, a layer of ice would cover the developing tray. Also the low temperatures ruined the developer. To insure purity, the water which had to be melted was filtered through charcoal."

Eric joined Anderson and his brother Pete at Lake Bennett in May, to wait for the spring thaw. Again Hegg set up an informal studio—this time in just a tent. The ice broke on May 30, and the men set out in two boats for the gold fields. By this time a fourth member had joined their party—a seaman by the name of Grant.

Anderson had equipped the Hegg boat with a dark room so that Eric could carry on with his photographic work.

After a busy season about the gold fields, E. A. Hegg made a hurried trip to New York to the Eastman Kodak Company for more film. When pictures of Chilkoot, White Pass, and nuggets and mines were shown in New York, the popu-lace went wild. For days they crowded Fifth Avenue for a sight of the pictures. Not until police on horseback arrived could order be re-stored.

Hegg returned to Dawson, where he was then located, sold his studio to Duclos and Larss, and in 1900 moved down the Yukon to Nome, always making pictures.

In moving from place to place, Hegg carried his photographic supplies in five gallon kerosene cans to insure safety. Putting the paper, and so forth, in the can, he labeled and weighed it, marking each can with its contents. Once when crossing the ice, his sled broke through, horse and all. But his supplies remained safe and dry.

In all, he spent twenty years in the North, part of which time he acted as official photog-rapher for the Guggenheim interests at Cordova. When he finally returned to the States he brought with him an indelible record of early Alaska and the Yukon. Many of his pictures found their way into histories. He operated studios in Fresno, California, for seven years. When he was in San Diego, he received an assignment to go to Hawaii. Hawaii offered many interesting experi-ences, one of which was to paint portraits of the Royal Family, for Hegg was also an accom-plished artist. But his old home and friends beckoned him and he returned finally to Belling-ham. Styles may change but brides are brides and babies have the same appeal, so he pros-pered in his photographic work. Mr. Hegg loved the great outdoors and he always interspersed his studio work with photographs of mountains, rivers, lakes, and trees. In time the walls of his studio in the Sunset Building were lined with his work. Then, in 1946, he sold his Bellingham studio and went to live with his son Roy in Cali-fornia. He did not live to see the publication of his photographs in book form; the first edition of *Klondike '98* appeared in 1949. Hegg died on December 13, 1948.

In sixty-five years of active work, he had seen many changes in photography. He remembered when wet plates were used instead of films, when pictures could be taken only in bright sunlight. Early in his career he had used albu-min paper, which had to be made up each morn-ing if the day showed signs of being bright enough for photographic work. The coating lasted but a few hours and had to be used at once. Dry plates followed wet plates. Then came cut film. Today, photography is simple compared to that of seventy years ago, but even by today's standards Hegg's results are enviable.

Concerning

Ethel A. Becker,

Author

Ethel Anderson Becker was herself a sourdough Klondiker of '98, and she has dedicated a lifetime of research to gathering authentic material on the Northland, particularly the Gold Rush to the Klondike. She was born in the State of Washington, at New Whatcom, later called Bellingham. These were days of logging with oxen, of trees cut ten feet from the ground because saws had not yet been made long enough to cut the big ones lower, of windjammers and the spicy smell of cedar sawdust and fir, of pioneer days as rugged as they were fascinating.

Etched in the author's memory since childhood is a trip up the White Pass Trail, riding now by tram, now by pack horse, or trudging behind to keep warm; of boarding the last boat of the season out of White Horse, bound for Dawson. Low water made travel slow and uncertain and the squatty stern-wheeler never missed a sandbar on the way to the Klondike. Ice was swirling by before the boat reached Dawson, and its passengers and cargo were brought in over a frozen Yukon.

The author's family lived on No. 16, Eldorado, where the father, P. B. Anderson, furnished wood from a receding forest for cribbing the shafts, thawing the frozen gravel, and building cabins and sluice boxes. The children, Ethel and Dewey and Clay, had their own little rocker where $14 was considered a good day's "work." She recalls:

"In our little fourteen-by-twenty-foot cabin we lived truly a pioneer life. The log cabin boasted one four-pane window and a floor. Most of the cabins at that time had no windows because glass was very expensive and scarce and they had no floors because the men were out grubbing for gold—but papa covered ours with poles split in half and laid flat side up. The roof was also of poles, covered with canvas and dirt. When mama saw that dirt roof she was glad she had brought garden seed with her — lettuce, radish, and onion seeds. These she planted on the roof in the spring and we had early vegetables (and vitamins) protected and hastened by the heat from the cabin.

"Below us in the valley were the mines, dumps of pay dirt, and piles of tailings. Flumes circled the hills and sluice boxes crisscrossed the valley between the dumps, carrying water to wash out the pay dirt. Through the winter men thawed and picked at the frozen ground deep in the shaft, hauled the pay dirt to the surface with a windlass, and dumped it in huge piles.

"Almost every day we played we were miners with our own little rocker. When we cleaned it out there was always a gathering of gold dust in the aprons inside. In climbing over a pile of tailings, Dewey found a flat yellow rock about the size of a dollar and as thin, plastered to the shale. When we washed the flat rock in a puddle, it proved to be a beautiful yellow nugget.

"Food was scarce that first winter. No one could foresee that thousands of sourdoughs would invade the Klondike land, many of whom were out of 'grub' when they arrived in Dawson. How then could they survive when no man had enough for himself? But our papa was still a hunter, and Rabbit Creek, or Bonanza, where the first big strike was made, was a rabbit heaven. Mother cleaned rabbits, rabbits, rabbits. What is more gruesome, more unappetizing than a skinned rabbit! But it was good food and we lived well. However, mama never ate rabbit after we left the Klondike.

"As the population increased it was no longer safe to leave gold in unlocked cabins. With Dawson fifteen or twenty miles away, this presented a real problem for miners working a long day and living in tents. Where could they safely leave their gold pokes? With mama, of course, for she never left the cabin. One after the other, men would approach her to keep their gold-filled pouches. The miners inked their names on their poke and when they had gone mama hid it under the straw-filled mattress on the bed. No one knew how much she had, but often dozens of fat moose-hide sacks lay around like so many plump sausages when she raised the mattress to make the bed or stash another gold poke into hiding.

"In 1902, we left the Klondike with its pioneering experiences and fabulous gold fields and returned 'outside' to Bellingham. We literally dripped nuggets. Mama had a long nugget watch chain which circled her neck and hung below her belt until it looped back to the watch at her waist. I had a nugget necklace. We had nugget rings and papa had a big nugget stick pin and watch fob.

"Most of those who took that stampede trail never found the pot of gold at the rainbow's end, but found instead riches more elusive perhaps than nuggets and gold dust, and more lasting in satisfaction. People bound by hardships and the need for one another develop bonds of loyalty and understanding that are never broken —bonds which grow more precious with the years."

————————

With the exception of primary schooling in the Klondike, Mrs. Becker received her education in Bellingham, graduating from the Bellingham State Normal School in 1913. Teaching, then marrying, and rearing two boys and two girls, filled the next years. Later she made Olympia, Washington, her home; then Vancouver, B. C., when she was caring for her mother. In recent years she moved to Seattle, where she now resides.

What began as a hobby, collecting early Alaska pictures, stories, and data, has resulted in a rare and rich knowledge of the Gold Rush to the Klondike. The desire to preserve this history, along with E. A. Hegg's remarkable collection of photographs, has been the purpose of this book, *Klondike '98*.